Precious few contemporary ministry resou
encouragement for pastors who know that the
in preaching and teaching" (1 Tim 5:17). Fra
been out of season for decades (see 2 Tim 4:2-

But *Pastoral Preaching: Building a People for God* by Conrad Mbewe is a welcome sign that the tide may be turning. Here is a truly valuable book about the pastor's preaching ministry – from the pen of a man who is supremely qualified to write on the subject.

Pastor Mbewe has faithfully served one congregation for nearly three decades, devoting himself "to the public reading of Scripture, to exhortation, to teaching" (1 Tim 4:13) with steadfast patience and sound, biblical doctrine. He is, in my judgment, one of the finest biblical preachers anywhere, known for his clarity, accuracy, thoroughness, courage, keen insight, and uncompromising faithfulness to the text of Scripture. This excellent book embodies all those qualities. It will fill a gaping void on the list of essential pastoral resources.

John MacArthur
Pastor, Grace Community Church, Los Angeles
President, The Master's College and The Master's Seminary, Los Angeles, USA

Conrad Mbewe has provided us with a most useful book, written from within an African context for preachers everywhere. The problems prevalent in churches and preaching today are brought to light and shown for what they are.

His concern is with how we "shepherd God's flock through God's Word," that is, how we preach in order to build the faith of those who have already been brought into the local church. He looks at why we preach, what we preach and how we preach, giving useful guidelines, encouragement and direction. The English is simple and straightforward, making this book an interesting and informative read which will benefit pastors of all ages and of all denominations in their study. If all pastors and churches were to follow the teaching in this book, then surely the life of the church would grow in numbers and in the faith!

Rev Benjamin A. Kwashi, PhD
Anglican Archbishop of Jos, Nigeria

Drawing on his decades-long experience in pastoral ministry in Africa, Conrad Mbewe has offered us an immensely readable book on what it takes to be a faithful minister of the gospel. Though grounded in Africa, his insights are applicable in all six continents and will come in handy for all who are called to pastoral ministry.

Pastoral Preaching is full of biblical insight to equip pastors for what must be one of the most crucial, and yet challenging, leadership callings in Africa today – the pastor in the local church. His adept treatment of the role of pastoral preaching is a good contribution to both church health and church growth. The church in Africa is growing very fast, and the growth often outpaces the development of new leaders to manage the growth. The result is that growth is often attended by errors of diverse sorts. Mbewe's book provides timely help for those at the coalface of managing the rapid spread of African Christianity. With the centre of gravity of Christian presence in the world shifting away from the West, it is all the more vital for African church leadership to be thoroughly equipped for their task. The future of Christianity, its integrity and credibility will be shaped in important ways by how African Christians steward it for future generations.

Not only does Mbewe make a compelling case for biblically sound pastoral preaching in the church, his eye goes beyond the walls of the church and envisages pastoral preachers who equip believers to be salt and light in their community. Africa is one of those places in the world where the charge could be made that "there are so many Christians and yet so little Christianity," judging by the limited impact of the faith on the vital indices that measure human flourishing in African societies.

Pastoral Preaching is for those who wish to take their ministry calling seriously and acquit themselves well as faithful servants of the Lord. I heartily commend it to fellow labourers whose charge is to feed the Lord's flock.

Rev Moss Ntlha
Pastor and General Secretary of the Evangelical Alliance of South Africa

Pastoral Preaching

Langham

PREACHING RESOURCES

Pastoral Preaching

Building a People for God

Conrad Mbewe

Langham
PREACHING RESOURCES

Copyright © 2017 by Conrad Mbewe

Published 2017 by Langham Preaching Resources
An imprint of Langham Creative Projects

Langham Partnership
PO Box 296, Carlisle, Cumbria, CA3 9WZ
www.langham.org

ISBNs:
978-1-78368-180-8 Print
978-1-78368-182-2 Mobi
978-1-78368-181-5 ePub
978-1-78368-183-9 PDF

Conrad Mbewe has asserted his right under the Copyright, Designs and Patents Act, 1988 to be
identified as the Author of this work.

All Scripture quotations, unless otherwise indicated, are taken from The Holy Bible, English
Standard Version. Copyright © 2001 by Crossway Bibles, a publishing ministry of Good News
Publishers. Used by permission. All rights reserved.

British Library Cataloguing in Publication Data
A catalogue record for this book is available from the British Library

ISBN: 978-1-78368-180-8

Cover & Book Design: projectluz.com

To the people of God at Kabwata Baptist Church who have authenticated everything I have written in this book by their own response to my pastoral preaching over the last thirty years.

CONTENTS

Acknowledgements

As this book goes to print, I am mindful that I have stood on the shoulders of many people in order to reach this point. It is only right that I should acknowledge those individuals who have played the most significant roles in this project. Unfortunately, I cannot name everyone, and can only mention those whose roles stand out like Mount Kilimanjaro in my mind.

I have received invaluable input from a group of pastors in Lusaka, Zambia, who met with me weekly to go through a chapter at a time as this book was being written. So let me thank Chipita Sibale, Kasango Kayombo, Clement Kaunda, Oswald Sichula, Wege Sinyangwe, German Banda, Curtis Chirwa, Kennedy Kawambale, and Saidi Chishimba for taking so much time to work with me on this project from beginning to end.

Our church pastoral interns in 2015 were also helpful during these discussions, especially as they asked the kind of questions that new pastors are likely to want answered in this book. The fact that they were from South Africa, Botswana, Tanzania, and Zambia ensured that the book is scratching where it is itching in different parts of Africa. So, Joshua Lungu, Michael Legodi, Simon Patilo, Ignatius Popolo, and Isaac Bipanda, thank you very much for your contribution to the making of this book.

Let me also thank the elders and deacons at Kabwata Baptist Church for giving me space in my pastoral work to be an author. They gave me a whole month off work in the course of the year to concentrate on this project. That enabled me to go and hide in the hills of Namibia for a whole week to do nothing but write. I am most grateful to Norman and Stephanie van Zyl for hosting me during that most productive week.

At Langham Literature, I am grateful to Pieter Kwant for pushing me into a form of writing I had never done before. This is the first book I have written without first presenting the contents to a live audience. It would not have been done if Pieter had not continued knocking on my door. I am also grateful to Dahlia Fraser and Isobel Stevenson for their editorial assistance. Where would we be without editors?

I am grateful to the management and faculty of Reformed Theological Seminary in Jackson, Mississippi, in the USA for allowing me to deal with the subject of pastoral preaching in their 2015 John Reed Miller lectures. I am equally grateful to the management and faculty of the Samara Centre for

Biblical Studies in Samara, Russia, for allowing me to use this material during their 2016 pastors' conference. In each case, I was able to use half of the chapters that make up this book as lecture material. Preparing these chapters for lecturing in an American and Russian context increased my confidence that although I have dressed the principles I am teaching in African clothes, they are of universal significance.

Lastly, I want to thank my wife, Felistas, and all our children for the time they gave me to concentrate on this project. It is not easy to have a husband and father who is absorbed with a writing project, because even when he is at home you can tell that he is still not with you. His mind is absorbed with the book that he has to finish. May God compensate you for having been deprived of a husband and father's attention.

Introduction

The people sitting in the pews listening to their pastor sometimes wish that they too could have the privilege of preaching. But very few realize how demanding preaching is. It is at the core of pastoral ministry, but what you see in the pulpit is only the tip of the iceberg. Since we do not have icebergs in Africa, I will change my illustration. What we see in the pulpit is the final thatching of a house. Prior to that a lot of work has gone into building the substructure and the superstructure of the house. Then there was the gathering of all the grass, twigs, and branches needed before the thatching work can begin. It is a lot of hard work.

Just as the goal of building a house is to produce a beautiful, usable home, so also the goal of pastoral preaching is to produce a people who know their God and are living lives that glorify him. Pastoral preaching must build a people for God. It is wonderful to see this happen when pastoral preaching has been done faithfully. The church will then be a place where the joy and peace of the Lord are present and where both the leaders and the ordinary church members show evidence of spiritual maturity. That is the type of church in which those who are waiting for a call to pastoral ministry long to serve! Yet this fruit does not come easily. It is the result of many years of faithfully preaching "the whole counsel of God" to the people of God (Acts 20:27).

It is because this fruit is so rare these days, especially here in Africa, that I have put pen to paper. Yet this is not an exclusively African problem. Many years ago while visiting Australia, John Stott was asked how he assessed the situation in the worldwide church since he had preached in so many places around the globe. Without hesitation, he stood up and wrote three words on the board: "Growth without depth." In other words, there was an increase in quantity without an equal increase in quality. People were getting converted and the church worldwide was growing, yet the people of God were not being helped to truly glorify God in their lives. That was the concern of John Stott as he looked at the worldwide church at that time.

Things have not changed; if anything, they have got worse. More and more pulpits are occupied by motivational speakers rather than preachers. Also, true preaching has given way to "deliverance" ministry. Pastors are treasured more for the deliverance prayers they conduct at the end of the church service than for the teaching they give in their sermons. Add to this the entertainment craze in today's world and you will understand why serious pastoral preaching is in short supply. The result is that we are producing Christians who lack true spiritual depth. Because they lack firm roots, they are easily swept away when cults come into town. They also fail miserably when it comes to handling the storms of life.

How can we who are pastors truly build a people for God? This is the question that I seek to answer in this book. Let me begin by saying that this is not a book on what colleges call "homiletics" (that is, the art of sermon preparation and delivery). There are many books out there on that subject. Rather, in this book I am addressing a number of key areas related to preaching in a pastoral context.

We will begin by looking at the difference between pastoral preaching and evangelistic preaching because we need to understand the role pastoral preaching plays in shepherding the people of God and what its primary focus should be. When farmers begin tilling their land in the spring, they know very well what work awaits them in the months ahead before they will see a harvest, and so they are able to keep on with their work. But many people enter pastoral ministry with only a vague idea about what work awaits them in pastoral preaching. Hence, they end up like goats, wandering around nibbling on one blade of grass after another until they get lost because they do not know where they ought to be going. And once the pastor is lost, the congregation is also lost. Therefore, it is vital that the primary pegs of pastoral preaching be deeply hooked into place in the minds of pastors at the start of their pastoral ministry if they are to keep their biblical bearings.

It is also important that pastors appreciate the context in which they will be exercising their ministry—the church of the Lord Jesus Christ. Mechanics who understand the context of their workshop are able to make the fullest use of the available tools. Otherwise, they will keep going elsewhere to get help that is only an arm's length away! The church is like that. The Lord Jesus Christ has engineered pastoral ministry and pastoral preaching to go together hand in glove. The church both benefits from pastoral preaching and aids pastoral preaching. Once pastors realize this, they will harness the church's full potential to help them in their work of preaching.

Another area that I address in this book is that of training. What kind of training best enables pastors to attain and maintain a preaching ministry that will build a people for God? There is the initial training that some pastors go through before they enter pastoral ministry. However, the church in Africa is growing so rapidly that the traditional system of formal training is unable to cope. In this book, I emphasize the role of pastors in training the next generation of pastors rather than leaving everything to Bible colleges. There are opportunities for ongoing training through pastors' groups or minister's fraternals, reading the right books, and listening to good pastoral preachers who are successful in their work.

One reason many pastors fail in the work of pastoral preaching is simply that they do not realize how challenging it is. There are real challenges in pastoral preaching, quite apart from the general challenges in pastoral ministry. In this book I concentrate exclusively on the former. I deal with the formidable and humanly impossible task of unhinging sin from human hearts. I also deal with the challenge of preaching well and relevantly. Your future as a pastoral preacher hangs on these. So, you need to know them and face them squarely if you are going to truly build a people for God in the long haul.

One reason there is such a lack of depth in the lives of believers even after they have sat under pastoral preaching for many years is the failure of pastors to make use of the whole Bible in their preaching. Do not get me wrong. Most pastors will quote well-known verses from across the whole range of Scripture when they preach. However, they do not preach from the whole Bible. Some prefer narrative passages; others prefer the teaching passages. Often they simply use these passages as pegs on which to hang their own thoughts in the form of topical sermons. I have sought to address this shortcoming by dealing with the full breadth of Scripture, giving a few pointers on how to handle the different parts so that in preaching from the various types of biblical writings a pastoral preacher can faithfully use them as God intended them to be used.

There is a modern idea that powerful pastoral preaching is the fruit of a special anointing of the Holy Spirit that some people have and others do not have, either because they did not seek it in the first place or because God simply did not want to give it to them and instead gave it to others. Nothing could be further from the truth. Hence, in this book I address the subject of power in pastoral preaching. Where does it come from? Yes, it is a fruit of the work of the Holy Spirit, but there is little that is strange or mystical about it. We need to be biblical even in seeking to be powerful pastoral preachers.

Finally, I discuss the rewards of faithful pastoral preaching. In light of the cost and sacrifice that often attends pastoral work, there is nothing better calculated to keep up our drooping spirits than a look at what awaits us at the finishing line. I deal with the rewards in this life and in the life to come. There is no work that is more gratifying than the work of pastoring the people of God. There is no part of that work that is more satisfying than pastoral preaching. Seeing its fruit in later years and in eternity will certainly prove that point more than anything else. I end the book on that glorious note!

As you read this book you will soon discover that my primary audience is pastors serving here in Africa. This is deliberate. Pastors in the Western world have so many Bible colleges and seminaries and so many books on pastoral ministry that to write for them would be like adding a drop to an ocean full of water. I would rather spend my energy giving water to those who have little or none. So, I have spent my time writing this book with fellow pastors in Africa in mind because they have very few resources that address this matter. I am seeking to scratch where very few are scratching.

Another reason for the focus on Africa is that this is the area in which I have laboured. They say, "It takes a thief to catch a thief." When I read books on pastoral ministry and preaching written by authors in the Western world, I appreciate the principles being taught but I often find the authors shooting over the heads of those who live in my own neighbourhood, who have not been exposed to the thought patterns and idioms of the Western world. If only those writers would trade in their long-range missiles for bows and arrows they might hit the mark. So, what I have done in this book is basically to take the same principles and clothe them in African attire.

That, by the way, also explains the brevity of this book. I could have easily doubled its length by quoting from authorities on pastoral preaching in the Western world. However, I am painfully aware that every extra page increases the cost of the book, and the average African pastor survives on very little. So, whatever I could leave out, I have left out in order to make the book as affordable as possible for my primary readership. I trust that those who want to read further on the subject of pastoral preaching will go on to buy other books once they have replenished their pockets.

Let me, however, quote one Western writer, Jim Shaddix, who says that there is a great need "for practical preaching help from a pastoral perspective in the tradition where preaching is a paramount and frequent event in the life of the local church."[1] These words expose the gap that I am seeking to fill in writing this book.

My only justification for daring to write on this topic is that I have laboured in pastoral preaching in the same church here in Africa for thirty years. I have seen the fruit of such preaching over time as a congregation of

---

1. Jerry Vines and Jim Shaddix, *Power in the Pulpit* (Chicago: Moody, 1999), 11.

God's people has grown both in quantity and quality. It has been exacting, and there have been a few times when I have wondered whether I am coming or going. Yet, when I look back over the years of pastoral preaching and see the fruit, I am convinced that this is the way to go. I have put my pen to paper because I want to share what the Lord has taught me as a practitioner of the art of pastoral preaching. I have learnt some of these lessons by making costly mistakes. Thankfully not too many lessons have been learnt that way!

The writing of this book has been a labour of love, though I initially felt like David when he was asked to fight Goliath while wearing Saul's armour. The request to write this book came from Langham Partnership and I readily accepted the challenge. It was not long before I realized that though I have written a number of books before, none of them had been written without first being presented to a live audience. This was going to be the first time for me to do so. And for two years I failed miserably! Finally, I remembered reading somewhere that Dr John Stott used to have a study group that helped him with his writing projects. So, I decided to ask a few local pastors to meet with me weekly to go through the chapters I was working on. (Their names are listed in the acknowledgements). That worked superbly! Their input was invaluable. They challenged some of my presuppositions, added extra thoughts, and advised me to move some things around. So, this book is a joint venture, though I take full blame for its shortcomings.

Section A

What Pastoral Preaching Is

1

Pastoral Preaching and Evangelistic Preaching

From the perspective of angels in heaven, there are only two kinds of people on this planet –Christians and non-Christians. Granted, we tend to notice much more variety than that because we see people through social and economic lenses. Thus we see rich and poor, educated and uneducated, good and bad, famous and unknown, powerful and vulnerable, male and female, etc. I am sure God's angels also see these differences, but such things are insignificant when it comes to our eternal destiny. What matters above everything else is whether a person is in Christ.

Preachers should have a similar perspective to angels. Our first concern should be whether our hearers are in Christ. Evangelistic preaching is needed to bring sinners into the kingdom. But we also have a second assignment: to help those who have come to Christ to grow spiritually. Achieving this goal requires pastoral preaching. Some may think that this distinction between evangelistic preaching and pastoral preaching is artificial, but Jesus himself acknowledged two types of preaching when he gave his Great Commission:

> All authority in heaven and on earth has been given to me. Go therefore and make disciples of all nations, baptizing them in the name of the Father and of the Son and of the Holy Spirit, teaching them to observe all that I have commanded you. And behold, I am with you always, to the end of the age. (Matt 28:18–20)

The Call to Evangelistic Preaching

The first task Jesus gave to his disciples was that of reproducing themselves by bringing people into the kingdom of God. They were to "make disciples."

How were they to do this? By preaching. The parallel renderings of the Great Commission in the other gospels spell this out very clearly, particularly when we recognize that the word translated "proclaim" in the ESV is translated as "preach" in many other versions. In the Gospel of Mark we read: "Go into all the world and proclaim the gospel to the whole creation. Whoever believes and is baptized will be saved, but whoever does not believe will be condemned" (Mark 16:15–16). Similar words are found in the Gospel of Luke: "Thus it is written, that the Christ should suffer and on the third day rise from the dead, and that repentance and forgiveness of sins should be proclaimed in his name to all nations, beginning from Jerusalem" (Luke 24:46–47).

Clearly God commands us to go all over the non-Christian world preaching the good news of Jesus and him crucified and calling people to repentance and faith in him. Those who respond to this call are to be initiated into localised colonies of faith called "the church." This initiation is what Jesus was referring to when he spoke about "baptizing them in the name of the Father and of the Son and of the Holy Spirit" (Matt 28:19).

Evangelistic preaching is needed because, according to the Bible, everyone on earth is in rebellion against God their maker. This is true even if they are sincere followers of some other religion. Africans in their traditional African religions are as much lost and rebellious as Asians in their mystical religions. They are worshipping a God they do not know and they insist on worshipping him in their own way. God is concerned about this and wants to correct it. He makes this correction by sending preachers to all peoples of the earth with the good news of salvation through Jesus Christ.

Preaching in Athens in the first century, the Apostle Paul said:

> Being then God's offspring, we ought not to think that the divine being is like gold or silver or stone, an image formed by the art and imagination of man. The times of ignorance God overlooked, but now he commands all people everywhere to repent, because he has fixed a day on which he will judge the world in righteousness by a man whom he has appointed; and of this he has given assurance to all by raising him from the dead. (Acts 17:29–31)

Paul was challenging erroneous thinking in the religion of the people in Athens and telling them that time was up! God was no longer going to tolerate this type of ignorance and was now demanding that all people everywhere abandon false forms of worship. He had unveiled his Son, Jesus Christ, as the way, the truth, and the life. He was now calling all people everywhere to submit to Jesus or be damned forever. Jesus who had died was now alive and was going to judge all human beings on the final day of judgment.

Like Paul, we as preachers must proclaim the gospel of repentance towards God and faith in the Lord Jesus Christ to all and sundry. We must not go only to those who claim to have no religion. We must go even to those who are sincere in their Christless religions and implore them to come to Christ in repentance and faith. It is not politically correct to do this, but it must be done if we are to be true to our commission.

Evangelistic preaching must wrestle with the consciences of unbelievers. It must go into the caves where they are hiding and smoke them out. How? By understanding the arguments and philosophies they use to blind their consciences to the fact that they are living in rebellion and sin. We must then show through logical argument that their positions are untenable. This is what Paul did when he told the people of Athens that the Creator does not live in buildings made by human hands and that they were guilty of idolatry, which God was commanding them to repent of.

It is because of the Great Commission that Christianity is unstoppable. The evangelistic task continues to result in the re-evangelization of every generation and the spread of Christianity into new territories as every generation passes the baton on to the next. Missionaries are being sent to places where the gospel has not yet taken root and new churches are being planted. Evangelistic meetings continue to be held in various places, calling young and old to put their trust in Christ as their personal Lord and Saviour.

When David Livingstone first came to Central Africa, there were no Christians here. In fact, Central Africa was an empty space on the world map. When he preached, there was often little or no visible effect and he was very discouraged. He wrote,

> I had been . . . in closer contact with heathenism than I had ever been before; and though all . . . were as kind and attentive to me as possible, . . . yet to endure the dancing, roaring, and singing, the jesting, anecdotes, grumbling, quarrelling and murdering of these children of nature, seemed more like a severe penance than anything I had before met with in the course of my missionary duties.[1]

---

1. David Livingstone, *Missionary Travels and Researches in South Africa*, 1857, chapter 12. Available as ebook #1039 from www.gutenberg.org.

However, he had hope that the preaching of later missionaries and pastors would bear more fruit because they would be building on the foundations laid by pioneer missionaries.

> Our work and its fruits are cumulative; we work toward another state of things. Future missionaries will be rewarded by conversions for every sermon. We are their pioneers and helpers. Let them not forget the watchmen of the night – us, who worked when all was gloom, and no evidence of success in the way of conversion cheered our paths. They will doubtless have more light than we, but we served our Master earnestly and proclaimed the same gospel as they will do.[2]

He was right. The work of evangelism is bearing a lot of fruit across Africa today!

This evangelistic enterprise must, however, continue until the earth is filled "with the knowledge of the Lord as the waters cover the sea" (Isa 11:9; Hab 2:14). Or, to use the words of the Lord Jesus Christ, "This gospel of the kingdom will be proclaimed throughout the whole world as a testimony to all nations, and then the end will come" (Matt 24:14). The spiritual combine harvester will have reaped worshippers for the true God of heaven across human history, and then the end will come. The choir of angels in heaven will be joined by voices from every tribe, language, people, and nation, brought together through the gospel.

As we think about pastoral preaching in this book, we must not forget about or overlook the importance of evangelistic preaching. We must not fill the church buildings with truth while error is allowed to multiply unchallenged outside. This will be self-defeating because the darkness outside will soon invade the church, as has often been the case in the Western world. The light of the gospel must spread outside the church buildings and go into every city and village. It must bring about a transformation of society as men and women are brought to repentance and faith in Christ.

---

2. Extract from David Livingstone's diary for Sunday, 19 June 1853, quoted by William Garden Blaikie, *The Personal Life of David Livingstone,* 1880. Available as Ebook #13262 from www.gutenberg.org.

The Call to Pastoral Preaching

A close look at the Great Commission of our Lord Jesus Christ shows that evangelistic preaching must lead into the work of pastoral preaching. Jesus went on to say that once those who are converted are initiated into localised colonies of faith, they are to be "[taught] to observe all that I have commanded you." This is what pastoral preaching is all about. It is the teaching of those who believe and are brought into the church. They are to be taught to obey everything that Jesus, their Lord and Saviour, said they should do.

The Christian life is real life. It is like human life. Once a baby is born, it needs a good home. That home should be hygienic, with enough good food, and plenty of tender, loving care. Being in the right kind of home is what will ensure proper growth. That is how it is with Christianity. New Christians must be initiated into "the household of God, which is the church of the living God, a pillar and buttress of the truth" (1 Tim 3:15). There, they must be fed with the pure milk of the word so that they can grow. That is exactly what the Apostle Peter wrote: "Like newborn infants, long for the pure spiritual milk, that by it you may grow up into salvation" (1 Pet 2:3). We will leave the matter of the local church here for now, because later on we will deal with the local church as the context of pastoral preaching.

Pastoral preaching assumes that the primary hearers are individuals who have personally repented of their sins and trusted in Christ as their Saviour and Lord. It supposes that those being addressed have experienced the regenerating work of the Holy Spirit and have begun to bear the fruit of obedience to God. Its understanding is that these individuals are indwelt by the Holy Spirit, who will be taking what is being taught to them regularly and using it in their lives for their spiritual growth. It also presupposes that they have been initiated into the localised body of believers called the local church through baptism.

It is clear that the apostles of our Lord Jesus Christ took this view. For instance, the Apostle Paul wrote to the Colossians saying, "Him we proclaim, warning everyone and teaching everyone with all wisdom, that we may present everyone mature in Christ. For this I toil, struggling with all his energy that he powerfully works within me" (Col 1:28–29). By using the plural in the phrase "we proclaim," Paul was making the point that this was not just his own personal agenda. This was the task given by the Lord Jesus Christ to all those whom he called to the preaching ministry. They were to labour to present everyone mature in Christ and this was to be done through pastoral preaching. To borrow Paul's words: "we proclaim . . . warning everyone . . . teaching everyone with all wisdom."

Later in the same letter, Paul tells the Colossians, "As you received Christ Jesus the Lord, so walk in him, rooted and built up in him and established in the faith, just as you were taught, abounding in thanksgiving" (Col 2:6–7). It is evident from this that the apostles did not think that becoming a Christian was the end of the process; rather, it was only the beginning. Once people became Christians it was important for them to begin walking in Christ in such a way that they would become rooted and built up in him and established in the faith. This was a fruit of being taught. Again, this is where pastoral preaching comes in. It is the means by which believers are helped to grow into maturity in their Christian lives.

It is reminiscent of the Old Testament journey of the Israelites into the promised land, isn't it? It was a journey. Leaving Egypt did not mean arriving in the promised land. They had a long journey ahead of them and during that journey they were often chastised by God because they sinned against him. Even after they arrived in the promised land, they still had a life to live, and they often went astray. God gave them Moses in the desert journey so that he would instruct them how to live in order to please God. Moses said to them, "See, I have taught you statutes and rules, as the LORD my God commanded me, that you should do them in the land that you are entering to take possession of it" (Deut 4:5). They needed to be taught so that they would live the kind of life that God wanted them to live. God wanted them to live wholly for him, despite being surrounded by idols. That is precisely the role of pastoral preaching. It is to help believers live the life that God wants them to live.

The Call to Both Evangelistic and Pastoral Preaching

Although I have made a clear distinction between evangelistic and pastoral preaching, I am not suggesting that pastors need to choose one over the other. Pastors are called to do both. Take Timothy for example. The Apostle Paul left him to pastor the church at Ephesus, that is, to take care of the believers there, yet he still said to him, "do the work of an evangelist, fulfil your ministry" (2 Tim 4:5). So, the two types of preaching are not necessarily mutually exclusive. In fact some sermons will fulfil both functions: evangelizing unbelievers and edifying believers. An evangelistic sermon can have an application for believers, and a sermon meant for believers can include an evangelistic appeal.

However, the point I want to make is that a church that survives only on evangelistic preaching every Sunday will end up with malnourished believers. As important as it is for us as preachers to bring people to Christ through our preaching, we must be aware that we also need to build up a people for God. This will largely be done by our pastoral preaching.

Discussion Questions

1. Why do you think it is important for a pastor to be clear about the distinction between evangelistic and pastoral preaching?

2. Look back over the sermons you have preached in the last two months. How many of them were evangelistic, how many were pastoral, and how many were both?

3. Where would you largely place your gifts as a preacher? Do you think you are called to be primarily an evangelistic preacher or a pastoral preacher – or could it be both?

2

Pastoral Preaching and Shepherding

One good way to understand an institution or activity is to reduce it to a single word or phrase – a word or phrase that captures something of its essence. When you have found the best word you can, you will know what that institution or activity is all about. For instance, you can reduce the game of football to simply the word, "goals." That is what football is all about. If you want to expand that further, perhaps you could say "scoring goals." That is what causes the adrenaline to flow. Everything gravitates towards goals. That is the focus.

What about pastoral preaching? What is the one word that best encapsulates what you are doing as a preacher when you are engaged in pastoral preaching? I would like to suggest that the one word is "shepherding." If I were to expand this word into a phrase it would be "shepherding God's flock through God's Word." Once you grasp this phrase, you will understand the core purpose of pastoral preaching. This is what God wants to see the Christian pulpit achieve on a weekly basis. The people of God need to be shepherded.

What is the work of a shepherd? It is primarily to ensure the health and safety of the sheep. Sheep are very vulnerable to diseases and wild animals, and they tend to stray and get lost. So shepherds take their sheep out of the kraal every morning and guide them to places where they can feed and find good clean water. They keep a close eye on the sheep to see whether any of them show symptoms of ill health. They also scan the surroundings for threats such as predators looking for a meal. When the day is over, the shepherd leads the flock back into the sheep pen, counting them to ensure they are all safely in for the night.

Pastors and Elders as Shepherds

When the Apostle Paul was bidding farewell to the elders of the church in Ephesus, he said to them, "Pay careful attention to yourselves and to all the flock, in which the Holy Spirit has made you overseers, to care for the church of God, which he obtained with his own blood" (Acts 20:28). The word translated "care" is the Greek word *poimaino,* which means "to shepherd." It includes the ideas of feeding and ruling. So the Apostle Paul was urging the elders of the church in Ephesus to do for Christians what a shepherd does for sheep.

Paul was not the only New Testament writer who used this picture of shepherds to describe the role of elders in the church. Peter did the same. He wrote, "So I exhort the elders among you, as a fellow elder and a witness of the sufferings of Christ, as well as a partaker in the glory that is going to be revealed: shepherd the flock of God that is among you" (1 Pet 5:1–2). So, the first leaders of the church summarized the role of elders in one word, "shepherding."

The fact that God's Word likens Christians to a flock of sheep suggests that there are some similarities between them. One is that Christians are as vulnerable in the spiritual world as sheep are in the physical world. Sheep tend to pick up diseases from the environment, wander off and get lost, and often end up as food for wild beasts. Christians also tend to pick up wrong ideas from friends and false teachers, which weaken them spiritually. They go astray and make shipwreck of their lives. To avoid this, they need to be looked after. That is the task of the elders in the church.

There was a recent example in South Africa of a pastor who told his congregants to go outside and eat grass. They ran outside and began to eat grass like cows. Many of them got sick. The same pastor later asked his congregants to drink petrol, claiming that he had the power to turn it into fruit juice. Again, many of them did so. In many African churches, pastors are defrauding church members of money and having sex with female members as a way of "cleansing" them from bad spirits. These activities are becoming so prevalent that they are attracting the attention of national governments, who are now trying to put an end to them. How can church members fall prey to such gimmicks? It is because of their spiritual vulnerability. Without proper pastoral care Christians will be weak and will easily fall prey to false teachers.

How does this shepherding role of pastors and elders fit in with pastoral preaching? The connection is the Word of God. We can summarize pastoral preaching as "shepherding" because the primary tool for this shepherding role is the Word of God as it is preached and taught and used in counselling.

While all church elders are shepherds of the church of God, some elders are called by Christ to the work of preaching and teaching, in which they concentrate on feeding the people of God through the Word of God. The Apostle Paul recognized this distinction when he told Timothy, "Let the elders who rule well be considered worthy of double honour, especially those who labour in preaching and teaching" (1 Tim 5:17). The work those in the second group are doing is pastoral preaching.[1]

The connection between shepherding and pastoral preaching is also brought home by the word "pastoral" itself. It is the adjective derived from the noun "pastor," which is actually the Latin translation of the Greek noun *poimen,* meaning "shepherd," which Paul uses in Ephesians 4:11.

The shepherd metaphor also helps to clarify the difference between evangelistic preaching and pastoral preaching. Evangelistic preaching is aimed at those who are not in the sheep pen. It is the instrument by which Christ brings them in. He once said, "I have other sheep that are not of this fold. I must bring them also, and they will listen to my voice. So there will be one flock, one shepherd" (John 10:16). As we engage in evangelistic preaching, Jesus calls his sheep out of the world into his fold. Once they are in his fold, pastoral preaching takes over. So, in that sense, pastoral preaching is aimed at those who have repented of their sins and put their trust in Jesus Christ as their Lord and Saviour. We have already covered this ground in the last chapter. However, it is helpful to see this again in light of this metaphor.

No doubt, the importance of caring for the sheep is something that Peter never forgot because Jesus instructed him to do it three times over! John records the conversation between Peter and Jesus, revealing Peter's heartfelt responses.

> When they had finished breakfast, Jesus said to Simon Peter, "Simon, son of John, do you love me more than these?" He said to him, "Yes, Lord; you know that I love you." He said to him, "Feed my lambs." He said to him a second time, "Simon, son of John, do you love me?" He said to him, "Yes, Lord; you know

---

1. My intention here is not to criticize the various forms of church government that have evolved over the centuries that do not regard the pastor (or minister) as one of the elders. I certainly do not intend to act like a wild cow that has strayed into someone's maize field! That would not be helpful. I am simply showing how the metaphor of shepherding enhances our understanding of pastoral preaching.

that I love you." He said to him, "Tend [literally, "shepherd"] my sheep." He said to him the third time, "Simon, son of John, do you love me?" Peter was grieved because he said to him the third time, "Do you love me?" and he said to him, "Lord, you know everything; you know that I love you." Jesus said to him, "Feed my sheep." (John 21:15–17)

Spiritual Shepherds Promised in the Old Testament

It is instructive to realize that this shepherding role was also spoken of in Old Testament times. For instance, in the wonderful Psalm 23, David speaks about what God did for him as his Shepherd:

> The LORD is my shepherd; I shall not want.
>> He makes me lie down in green pastures.
> He leads me beside still waters.
>> He restores my soul.
> He leads me in paths of righteousness
>> for his name's sake.
> Even though I walk through the valley of the shadow of death
>> I will fear no evil,
> for you are with me;
>> your rod and your staff,
>> they comfort me. (Ps 23:1–4)

We also find that when God complained about the failure of the various classes of teachers in Israel – priests, prophets, scribes, and so on – to give his Word faithfully to his people, he referred to them as shepherds who had transgressed against him and caused his flock to be scattered (Jer 2:8; 10:21; 23:1–2; Ezek 34:1–6). Then, when God was promising to give his people true teachers, he again used the shepherd metaphor, saying, "I will give you shepherds after my own heart, who will feed you with knowledge and understanding" (Jer 3:15). Or, as he puts it later, "I will set shepherds over them who will care for them, and they shall fear no more, nor be dismayed, neither shall any be missing, declares the LORD" (Jer 23:4).

The first of these shepherds is Jesus, who referred to himself as the Good Shepherd in John 10. He is the fulfilment of the Old Testament promise that God himself would come and shepherd his people (Ezek 34:11–24). Jesus also applied the shepherd metaphor to himself when he quoted the prophecy,

"Strike the shepherd and the sheep will be scattered" (Matt 26:31; quoting Zech 13:7).

As we have seen, Jesus commanded Peter to feed his sheep, and Peter picks up on this idea when he describes Jesus as "the chief Shepherd" who does his shepherding work through his under-shepherds (1 Pet 5:1–4, especially verse 4). These under-shepherds are the elders of the church, especially those whose work is preaching and teaching. As under-shepherds, they are expected to imitate the chief Shepherd, that is, they are to follow the example of Jesus Christ. His shepherding duties are described in Ezekiel 34:11–24 as involving searching for his straying sheep and rescuing them, feeding them in good, rich pasture, binding up the injured and strengthening the weak. What shepherds do in physical terms is what pastors should do in spiritual terms.

Shepherding through Pastoral Preaching

It is primarily but not exclusively through pastoral preaching that pastors restore straying believers, feed the people of God, and strengthen those who are weak. In short, it is primarily by using the Word that they fulfil their shepherding role. The Apostle Paul, referring to Jesus' gifts to his church wrote, "He gave the apostles, the prophets, the evangelists, the shepherds and teachers, to equip the saints for the work of ministry, for building up the body of Christ, until we all attain to the unity of the faith and of the knowledge of the Son of God, to mature manhood, to the measure of the stature of the fullness of Christ" (Eph 4:11–13).

Notice in this passage that the ongoing preaching in the church is meant to produce equipped, built-up, united, knowledgeable, mature believers – people who have attained "to the measure of the stature of the fullness of Christ." Paul did not refer to miracle workers or tongues speakers or those with administrative gifts but to those with preaching gifts, and among them he mentions "the shepherds." His words underscore the point that it is through what we are calling pastoral preaching that the church is to be shepherded. It is vital to remember this, especially in Africa today, as deliverance sessions are fast taking centre stage in church worship services. One new pastor has complained that his church members are not even listening to the preaching any more. They are interested in the deliverance sessions afterwards at which he prays for their marriages to be restored and their businesses blessed.

I am not saying this to disparage other gifts and needs in the church. They all have their place. After all, a body is not simply a mouth; it also has hands and feet. For the purpose of feeding, the mouth is the most important. For the purpose of hearing, the ear is the most important. For the purpose of seeing, the eyes are the most important. And for the purpose of walking the feet are the most important. Similarly, for the purpose of shepherding the people of God into maturity, the pastoral preaching gift that Jesus has given to his church is the most important.

It is very fitting then, that the instructions on how to shepherd the people of God are found in what we call the Pastoral Epistles (1 and 2 Timothy, Titus). Before the Apostle Paul died, he instructed Timothy to carry out his shepherding work faithfully: "I charge you in the presence of God and of Christ Jesus, who is to judge the living and the dead, and by his appearing and his kingdom: preach the word; be ready in season and out of season; reprove, rebuke, and exhort, with complete patience and teaching" (2 Tim 4:1–2). That was how Timothy was going to fulfil his call as shepherd of the people of God.

Pastoral preaching plays a unique role and must take centre stage in the life of the church, especially during the worship services. So it is of great concern that today in many churches across Africa, entertainment has taken the place of pastoral preaching. Pastors see themselves more as entertainers than shepherds. As a result, many Christians are spiritually weak and vulnerable to false teachings. The error is obvious. The sheep are telling shepherds what they want and, in order to keep them coming, the shepherds are obeying them. This is precisely what the Apostle Paul warned Timothy about when he wrote, "For the time is coming when people will not endure sound teaching, but having itching ears they will accumulate for themselves teachers to suit their own passions, and will turn away from listening to the truth and wander off into myths. As for you, always be sober-minded, endure suffering, do the work of an evangelist, fulfil your ministry" (2 Tim 4:3–5). Paul was expecting Timothy to fulfil the work of a faithful and true shepherd. We must do the same today through faithful pastoral preaching.

Discussion Questions

1. In which ways have you found the biblical concept of shepherding helpful in focusing your mind on what you should be doing in your pastoral work?

2. How can you use the shepherding metaphor to counsel a pastor who is being tempted to resort to entertainment instead of biblical preaching to grow his church?

3. Since few of us are farmers today, can you think of a metaphor for pastoral preaching that would be more helpful than "shepherding" in your context?

4. Think about the last few sermons you have preached in your church. What aspect of shepherding did they fulfil?

3

The Focus of Pastoral Preaching

Under-shepherds care for sheep that belong to someone else. They must never forget this. Their aim must always be to do their work in a way that pleases the owner of the sheep. After all, that is why they were hired. So, while they are working, each of them needs to keep one eye on the owner of the sheep. What about the other eye? That should be on kept on the sheep. This is because the condition of the sheep is what will produce the smile on the owner's face. If some sheep are sick or missing due to a shepherd's negligence, the owner will not be impressed.

What will under-shepherds be looking for as they keep their eyes on the sheep? First, they will be on the watch for any early symptoms of ill health, such as limping, lagging behind the rest of the flock and a lack of interest in eating. These are tell-tale signs that all is not well. Next, the under-shepherds will be focused on finding good grass and clean water for the sheep. Finally, while the flock are grazing the shepherds will be making sure that none of the sheep are wandering off and getting lost or falling prey to wild beasts.

If you ever had to care for cattle, sheep or goats before you became a pastor, you will be nodding your head in agreement with all this.

So, what about the shepherds whom we call pastors? What should be their primary focus as they shepherd the people of God through pastoral preaching?

The Glory of God

Just as under-shepherds are concerned about pleasing the owner of the sheep, so pastors must be concerned about pleasing God as they look after those he has placed in their care. But to be able to please him, they need to understand his purpose. Why does God even care to have sheep in the first place? In other words, what is the ultimate purpose of God's plan of salvation?

The answer is that God wants to be glorified through the salvation of sinners. So salvation itself is not the primary goal; it is the means to an even more glorious goal, which is to bring him glory. When the angels announced the birth of the Lord Jesus, they sang, "Glory to God in the highest, and on earth peace among those with whom he is pleased" (Luke 2:14). In salvation, glory goes to God and peace comes to us. Thus the glory of God should be a primary focus of pastoral preachers.

Even when Isaiah prophesied the coming of the Messiah into the world, and the way in which God would put his Spirit upon him, he did not lose sight of the fact that God was going to do all this for his own glory. He wrote, "The Spirit of the Lord GOD is upon me, because the LORD has anointed me to bring good news to the poor . . . that they may be called oaks of righteousness, the planting of the LORD, that he may be glorified" (Isa 61:1, 3).

Let us take a few steps back and ask, what does it mean to glorify God? It means to bring him pleasure by doing things that truly acknowledge his splendour as God. In other words, we are to give thanks to God for giving us all we are and have, and we are to worship God by acknowledging that he is worthy to receive from us all we are and have. That is how we glorify God.

Nonbelievers do not live for the glory of God. They glorify created things rather than the Creator (Rom 1:25). Even when they mingle with the people of God during church services, their primary question is, "Am I enjoying myself?" If the answer is in the negative, they may not show up the following week.

When this life is over all of us, believers and nonbelievers alike, will glorify God. The Bible says, "God has highly exalted him and bestowed on him the name that is above every name, so that at the name of Jesus every knee should bow, in heaven and on earth and under the earth, and every tongue confess that Jesus Christ is Lord, to the glory of God the Father" (Phil 2:9–11). God will ultimately be glorified!

But our goal should be to see God glorified among his people in this life. We should want to see God's people live their lives at home, at work or at church in such a way that God will find pleasure in them. This is why Jesus came – to bring glory to God by saving a people for himself. He has given the church pastors so that his people's capacity to bring glory to God can be enhanced. So, we as pastors should be constantly asking the question, "Is my preaching producing lives that are glorifying God?"

The Health of the People of God

Just as under-shepherds keep one eye on pleasing the owner of the sheep and the other on the health of the sheep, so pastors must focus on two main goals in ministry: the glory of God and the health of the people of God. These are two sides of the same coin. The former is only achieved when the latter is achieved. God will only be glorified when the people of God are in good spiritual health.

The people of God will only be healthy if the pastoral preaching they receive focuses on the five key areas discussed below.

A Comprehensive View of the Gospel

Pastoral preaching must help believers gain a comprehensive view of the content of the gospel. At the point of their conversion, there may have been only one gospel truth that gripped them, and this truth brought them to Christ for salvation. Maybe they felt worthless and unloved, and the gospel opened to them the height and depth and length and breadth of the love of God in Christ Jesus. Like a flower experiencing the warmth of the sun, they opened up and the Sun of Righteousness sent his healing rays into their souls with powerful saving effect. To them, that is now the beginning and end of the gospel message – it is all about a God who *loves* the unlovable.

Or maybe they were rebellious sinners and the gospel's warnings and offers of divine amnesty were heard with deafening decibels until they came out of their spiritual rebellion with their AK47s, as it were, in the air. To them, that is now the beginning and end of the gospel message – it is all about a God who *pardons* hell-deserving rebels.

Neither of these two groups of Christians has a panoramic view of the gospel. They both need to come to a deeper appreciation of it. In the same way, we all need to learn more about the saving work of Christ, the Son of God, in his pre-existent life, his humiliated life, and his glorified life. Believers need to be taught how the death, burial, and resurrection of the Lord Jesus Christ are the apex of his saving work and they need to know how all this relates to his ascension and position at the right hand of God. We all need to see that our experience of salvation is only a drop in an ocean of amazing grace, until we too can understand why Charles Wesley wrote in 1738,

> Tis mystery all, the Immortal dies!
> Who can explore such strange design?

In vain the firstborn seraph tries
    To sound the depths of love divine.
Tis mercy all! Let earth adore;
    Let angel minds inquire no more.

Christians also need to learn about the various fruits of this saving work of Christ, including regeneration, justification, adoption, sanctification, and glorification. I have never forgotten how as a young man in my early twenties, I stumbled across J. I. Packer's book *God's Words* and studied each of these concepts.[1] The impact that exercise had on me is indescribable. I felt as if I had been born again – again! These are all biblical words. Like women coming from the river carrying pails of refreshing water on their heads, each of these gospel words brings refreshment to our souls as we make our way through this weary world.

Paul and the other writers of the letters in the New Testament took time to explain the gospel to the first-century believers. The letter to the Romans is a classic example! We must do the same in our pastoral preaching. We must regularly explain important biblical concepts so that the people of God are confirmed in their faith and do not have to rely solely on their feelings, which change from day to day. That is why many young believers struggle with assurance of salvation. They have not understood that salvation is not based on feelings but on the unchanging promises of God that are anchored in the finished work of Christ on the cross, his ongoing work at the right hand of the Father in heaven, and the mighty workings of God's Spirit in our hearts.

Pastoral preaching should give us all a fuller understanding of the gospel and deepen our love for it so that we are eager to share it with others.

A Working Knowledge of the Bible

Pastoral preaching ought to help God's people to develop a working knowledge of the Bible. This applies not only to pastors working in urban centres but also to those whose congregations are in rural villages.

Although we refer to the Bible as a book, it is more like a library with sixty-six books. Granted, some of the books are very short, but when you read them you soon discover that they contain a wealth of material. They are like condensed milk, which packs a lot of goodness into a small can! That is

---

1. Re-issued as *18 Words: The Most Important Words You Will Ever Know* (Fearn, Scotland: Christian Focus, 2008).

how the Bible is. As we meditate upon it, we discover that its contents can fill the biggest libraries in the world.

Christians need to have a working knowledge of this library of books so that they are able to make good use of it when they need to know the mind of God concerning situations they may be facing. This is not as simple as it may sound because the Bible contains many different types of writing. There are history books, poetic wisdom books, prophetic books, and books that are essentially letters written to various churches and individuals. And the books are arranged in two major sections, called the Old Testament and the New Testament. The Old Testament points forward to Jesus' first coming, and the New Testament tells us about his first coming and points to his second coming. Pastoral preaching should help believers to find their way through this maze so that wherever they are in the Bible they will not get lost but will draw appropriate lessons for their own growth and maturity. They will learn to do this as they listen to good pastoral preaching that respects the contexts in which texts are found.

Despite the Bible having so many different sections, it is essentially one book because it has one theme; namely, the saving work of God through Jesus Christ. Believers need to be helped to have a Christocentric interpretation of the Bible. Jesus once challenged his adversaries during his days on earth, saying, "You search the Scriptures because you think that in them you have eternal life; and it is they that bear witness about me" (John 5:39). He was telling them that the whole Bible was about him.

He made the same point to his own disciples after his resurrection, when he opened their minds so that they could understand the Scriptures. Beginning with those whom he met on the road to Emmaus (Luke 24:13–27), and then with others (Luke 24:36–49), Jesus taught that the Scriptures spoke of him from the first page to the last. Now, if that was true concerning the Old Testament (which is what Jesus was referring to), how much more must it be true of the New Testament, which was written in response to his first coming? So, good pastoral preaching should be Christocentric, revealing Jesus Christ in the message of the whole Bible.

An Appreciation of Sound Doctrine

Pastoral preaching ought to help believers gain an appreciation of the whole counsel of God. Look at how the Apostle Paul described his ministry in Ephesus when talking to the elders of the church there: "Therefore I testify to you this day that I am innocent of the blood of all, for I did not shrink from declaring to you the whole counsel of God" (Acts 20:26–27). He must have said this with a sense of gratitude for a successful ministry.

What did Paul mean by "the whole counsel of God"? He must have been referring to all truths that God has revealed in Scripture – truths that are sweet and those that are sour due to our worldliness, truths that are fashionable and those that are unpalatable. That was why the Apostle Paul spoke in terms of "not shrinking." Preachers often shrink from talking about biblical truths that people do not want to hear. But preachers who do not proclaim the whole truth produce slanted and half-baked Christians who fail to live God-glorifying lives.

Another way of looking at this involves using a more modern phrase. Pastoral preaching must impart a sound systematic theology to the people of God. This does not mean that pastors must teach doctrine as is done in Bible colleges. Rather, this systematic understanding of God's truth must emerge as they preach through various passages of the Bible. There must be a doctrinal emphasis so that God's people develop a biblical view of God, creation, human beings, history, sin, redemption in Christ, salvation applied by the Holy Spirit, the church, the state, missions, the second coming of Christ, and so on. Although these may appear to be separate topics, believers must know how they interrelate and combine to form one reality. Pastoral preaching helps believers to develop a biblical, God-centred and gospel-saturated worldview.

The Apostle Paul explained that this was why Jesus Christ gave preachers and teachers to the church. We saw in the last chapter that "he gave the apostles, the prophets, the evangelists, the shepherds and teachers, to equip the saints for the work of ministry, for building up the body of Christ, until we all attain to the unity of the faith and of the knowledge of the Son of God, to mature manhood, to the measure of the stature of the fullness of Christ" (Eph 4:11–13). Note that these preaching and teaching gifts were given to bring believers to "the unity of the faith and of the knowledge of the Son of God."

When the Bible speaks of "the faith" (i.e. "faith" with the definite article "the" before it), it is referring to the body of truth that makes up the Christian faith. It is "the faith that was once for all delivered to the saints" (Jude 1:3). It is referring to Christian teaching or sound doctrine. The Apostle Paul is, therefore, saying that God gave preachers and teachers as gifts to his church to help believers come to a common understanding of Christian doctrine.

Why did God do this? A working knowledge of the Bible and an appreciation of sound doctrine will help believers to grow spiritually and avoid being misled by the many false teachings that are so widespread all around them. As the African proverb states, "When the roots are deep, there is no reason to fear the wind." Let us allow the Apostle Paul to speak for himself. He said God gave preachers and teachers to the church "so that we may no longer be children, tossed to and fro by the waves and carried about by every wind of doctrine, by human cunning, by craftiness in deceitful schemes. Rather, speaking the truth in love, we are to grow up in every way into him who is the head, into Christ" (Eph 4:14–15).

An Understanding of Godly Living

Pastoral preaching must help believers to see how God wants them to live in all areas of their lives – in their homes, in the workplace, in the church, and in the world. Pastoral preaching encourages believers to live godly lives in conformity to the standards that God has set for them. This grows out of the sound doctrine that they have been taught. We can see this clearly in Paul's letter to Titus, where he begins by saying, "But as for you, teach what accords with sound doctrine" (Titus 2:1), and then goes on to tell Titus to instruct older men, older women, younger men, and others, in how they must live in order to please God. For instance, "Older men are to be sober-minded, dignified, self-controlled, sound in faith, in love, and in steadfastness. Older women likewise are to be reverent in behaviour, not slanderers or slaves to much wine" (Titus 2:2–3).

Paul wants Titus to follow his own example in the letters he wrote to various churches. In those letters, he would write about some important Christian truth, and then say "therefore . . ." and spell out the implications of this truth for how they went about their daily lives (see, for example, Rom 12:1; 15:7; 1 Cor 4:5; Gal 5:1; Col 3:5). In his pastoral preaching, Titus must also use this famous "therefore."

Believers need encouragement to apply doctrine because often the environment around them does not encourage a Christian lifestyle, and is even hostile to it. The world has a culture that is godless and rebellious. Men and women insist on their "rights," but their insistence is often simply a thin veneer covering a militant self-determination that is against God's moral law. Although Christians' hearts have been cleansed from rebellion, they do not realize how much the world's culture still dominates their thinking. It remains a very big blind spot. Christians need regular soaking in the Word of God for that godless culture to be washed out of their thinking.

For instance, in many cultures in Africa, polygamy is normal. The more powerful a man is financially and politically, the more wives he accumulates. Wives are treated as though they are possessions. When a man is converted and sits under pastoral preaching, he soon learns that his wife is his equal before God and that God wants marriage to be between one man and one woman. He is also taught how a godly husband is supposed to view and treat his wife. He is to love his wife as Christ loved the church. As he wrestles with the implications of this, it totally transforms his relationship with his wife.

Another important area for regular instruction is how believers ought to live in the church. This is a whole new dimension that they only really experience at a spiritual level after their conversion. Even if they were going to church before they become Christians, they will have wrong perceptions. They need to realize, for instance, that there is no place for tribalism and social classes in the church. New believers will also need to realize that the church is neither the building in which they meet on Sundays nor the worship service, as important as these may be. The church is the people of God who covenant to live, worship, and serve God together. The Bible is full of "one another" passages, which need to be absorbed into the lifestyles of believers. Christians also need to be taught about the time and financial commitments they will need to make to the body of Christ. Pastoral preaching is the way we teach such things.

A Conviction about the Good Fight

Pastoral preaching should reveal to believers that they will have to fight the "good fight" for the rest of their earthly lives. Spiritual growth does not take place in a spiritually hygienic environment. Christians have a fallen world to contend with. We have already spoken about the culture of idolatry and rebellion that surrounds believers. It continually seeks to force them to conform to its ways, which is exactly what the Apostle Paul urged believers not to do (Rom 12:2).

Not only do Christians have to contend with the fallen world, they also have to contend with their own fallen natures, which are still averse to the levels of holiness and commitment to God that he demands in his Word. Overcoming this aversion is the only way to true joy and peace with God. The Bible says, "But I say, walk by the Spirit, and you will not gratify the desires of the flesh. For the desires of the flesh are against the Spirit, and the desires of the Spirit are against the flesh, for these are opposed to each other, to keep you from doing the things you want to do" (Gal 5:16–17). Pastoral preaching will teach God's people how to walk by the Spirit so that they do not gratify the cravings of their fallen nature.

Finally, pastoral preaching will point out to believers that the devil (also called Satan in the Bible) is real. He is a deceiver. He uses the enticing nature of the world and the cravings of our sinful natures in a very subtle way to trap us and make us fall. Remember, he is the one who brought about the fall of Adam and Eve when they were in a perfect world and had perfect natures. We are more vulnerable to his tricks than they were! God's people need to resist the devil in precisely the same way that Jesus did when he was tempted in the desert for forty days, that is, we resist by knowing and obeying God's Word (Matt 4:1–11). This note will need to be sounded again and again in pastoral preaching to protect God's people from straying.

To Sum Up

A working knowledge of the Bible, an appreciation of sound doctrine, an understanding godly living, and having a conviction about the need to fight the good fight of the faith helps believers to know how to handle the many and varied situations that will come up in their lives.

The rapid pace of urbanization in many countries has provided fertile ground for confusion and abandonment of values. In Africa, people are wrestling with traditional issues such as witchcraft, superstition, widow cleansing, polygamy and tribalism as well as with newer issues such as AIDS, unemployment, poverty, corruption and child abuse. Church leaders cannot always be available to answer questions from believers. However, where believers have sat under good pastoral preaching, their minds are trained to work from biblical principles and deal with these issues and the situations that arise from them in a way that truly glorifies God.

Discussion Questions

1. Why do you think it is important to make the glory of God your first and most important of focus as a pastor?

2. What are some of the areas on which your preaching has focused? Have you covered the areas dealt with in this chapter?

3. Preachers of the prosperity gospel focus primarily on two areas – health and wealth. What can you say about that in the light of what you have learnt from this chapter?

4. It is said that Christianity in Africa is a mile wide but only an inch deep. How do you think that the kind of pastoral preaching discussed in this chapter can remedy that?

Section B

Where Pastoral Preaching Is Done

4

Pastoral Preaching Depends on the Church

When you think of doctors at work, you think of the hospital as the context in which they attend to the sick. When you think of lawyers practising, you think of them in the context of a law court defending a client or establishing a case against someone. When you think of carpenters plying their trade, you visualize a workshop with pieces of wood all around and some finished products in a corner. When you think of chiefs, you think of the place from which they rule. For every job there is an appropriate place or setting. The place provides the context in which practitioners carry out the work that needs to be done. So, what is that right context for pastors as they carry out their preaching?

That context is the church – the local church. Pastoral preaching should naturally take place within the four walls of church buildings – or wherever believers are gathered together to worship God. This was implied in the words of the Great Commission:

> Go therefore and make disciples of all nations, baptizing them in the name of the Father and of the Son and of the Holy Spirit, teaching them to observe all that I have commanded you. And behold, I am with you always, to the end of the age. (Matt 28:19–20)

Notice the process. When sinners become disciples of Jesus, they are to be initiated into the local church through baptism. After that, they are to be taught to observe all that Jesus commanded. That is what pastoral preaching is about. It teaches those who have been brought into the local church.

Everyone who becomes a Christian should be encouraged to join a local church. It is the context in which they will be helped to grow in their Christian lives. Jesus did not leave his people to simply wander around as individuals and survive somehow until they go to heaven. No, he left them to be cared for by church elders. It is because of this that the Apostle Peter wrote:

> So I exhort the elders among you, as a fellow elder and a witness of the sufferings of Christ, as well as a partaker in the glory that is going to be revealed: shepherd the flock of God that is among you, exercising oversight, not under compulsion, but willingly, as God would have you; not for shameful gain, but eagerly; not domineering over those in your charge, but being examples to the flock. And when the chief Shepherd appears, you will receive the unfading crown of glory. (1 Pet 5:1–4)

Local churches are no accident; they exist by God's design. That was how Jesus wanted his disciples to be looked after. These disciples are the flock the elders are to shepherd. They are to be taught everything that Christ has commanded (Matt 28:20). Through their teaching and the example of mature believers – especially the church elders – Christians will learn how to live in a way that pleases God. Local churches are, therefore, nurturing grounds for believers.

But the benefits do not only flow in one direction. I know that we usually only think of how pastoral preaching benefits churches, but in this chapter I want to look at the various ways in which the church benefits pastors by providing the right setting or context for pastors to "ply their trade."

As we look at how the church benefits pastoral preaching, you may think that I am dealing with the whole of pastoral ministry and have forgotten that this book is about pastoral preaching. But pastoral preaching is part of pastoral ministry. As often as possible, I will emphasize pastoral preaching, but every so often I will refer to the wider pastoral ministry within which pastoral preaching is done.

The Church Nurtures Future Pastors

The most important benefit pastoral preaching gets from the church is that the church provides a place where future pastors are nurtured, just as young plants are nurtured in a nursery bed. We often think that Bible colleges and seminaries are the nursery beds for future pastors. To some extent we are correct. Bible colleges and seminaries have their place. They specialize in training those who are to spend their lives in spiritual ministries, including pastoring and preaching. However, they are not the primary nursery bed. That honour belongs to the church.

Paul wrote to Timothy, who at that time was pastoring the church in Ephesus, and told him, "What you have heard from me in the presence of many witnesses entrust to faithful men who will be able to teach others also" (2 Tim 2:2). Paul was not telling Timothy to start a Bible college. Rather, he was asking him to pay special teaching to those in the church who had the gifts of teaching and preaching. Timothy's pastoral responsibilities included ensuring that the church was nurturing future teachers.

In many African villages, you will find that every homestead includes a small circular structure consisting of vertical poles surmounted by a thatched roof. These *insakas* have no walls. They are where the head of the homestead spends time with his family, reciting folklore that has been passed on over the ages and educating his children, especially his sons, about life. It is in these *insakas* that young men are prepared for the responsibilities of adult life. The coming of Western-style schools in the villages has not done away with these *insakas* because they play a critical role in passing on the culture of the people. In the same way, the coming of Bible colleges should never do away with the role of the church in nurturing future preachers.

As we shall see in chapter 7, this nurturing begins as young believers sit under pastoral preaching. They see a good preacher at work. They are exposed to the preacher's hard work and integrity as the Scriptures are expounded and applied to the lives of the listeners. They listen as the preacher wrestles with their consciences. They see how lives are shaped, families are nurtured, and whole communities are transformed through this kind of preaching. They resolve in their hearts that if God ever opens a door of ministry for them, they will labour in the same way.

These are the people Paul was telling Timothy to nurture. As pastors, we too are to scan the congregation for those who are faithful and have teaching abilities so that we can give special attention to improving their teaching skills. Through one-on-one discipleship and small group training sessions, we should seek to nurture those in the church who show promise as teachers and preachers. In Africa where the church is growing exponentially – faster than Bible colleges are being established – this may be the only form of training that most future pastors will have for some time to come.

The Church Calls Pastors

Another way in which the church benefits pastoral preaching is that the church is the body that calls pastors to their work. Different denominations have different ways of doing this. Some use an episcopal system, others a presbyterian system, still others call pastors through congregational votes. Whatever system is used, whether bishops, synods and presbyteries, or a congregational vote, it is still the church that calls pastors into their work. They do not call themselves. Even if individuals are convinced that God has called them into pastoral work, the church must accept them before they can exercise their ministry.

This was the difficulty that the Apostle Paul faced after his conversion and call to the apostolic ministry. Because he had been a persecutor of the church, everyone ran away from him. For a while he exercised his gift evangelistically to the outside world, but it took some time before he was able to use it inside the church. It was Barnabas, the son of encouragement, who finally broke through this phobia. Here is the account of what happened:

> And when he had come to Jerusalem, he attempted to join the disciples. And they were all afraid of him, for they did not believe that he was a disciple. But Barnabas took him and brought him to the apostles and declared to them how on the road he had seen the Lord, who spoke to him, and how at Damascus he had preached boldly in the name of Jesus. So he went in and out among them at Jerusalem, preaching boldly in the name of the Lord. (Acts 9:26–28)

Yes, it was only after the church accepted Paul that he was able to go "in and out among them . . . preaching boldly in the name of the Lord." That is an important part of the benefit that preachers get from the church. Later, Paul was given the right hand of fellowship by the other apostles and assigned to give leadership to the church's thrust into the Gentile world while Peter gave leadership in the Jewish world (see Gal 2:1–10).

It is a great affirmation of your faith when the church acknowledges the direction in which you think God is calling you. Your fellow believers are the ones who have been listening to you as you have taught among them in an unofficial capacity. They are the ones who have trained you. They are now the ones who are calling you to occupy a demanding and distinguished office among them. It is a great honour. It is a great responsibility. It is a great affirmation that God is indeed calling you to this work.

Over the past twenty years there has been a spate of new "ministries" arising from church splits. Usually, the split was because individuals were thinking more highly of themselves than they ought. They did not wait for God's timing. Not wanting to work under the leadership of others any longer, they took a few church members and appointed themselves as pastors of their own churches. Sometimes they gave themselves high-sounding titles like "Apostle" or "Prophet." This is a very unhealthy situation. It has left churches vulnerable because there are no accountability structures. The leader is self-appointed and does not report to anyone. That is dangerous. What is needed is a proper understanding of the role of the church in calling pastors to their work.

The Church Pays Pastors

Yet another great benefit that pastoral preaching gets from the church is remuneration. I know that this is not always the case. Some churches, especially those in rural areas, do not have the means to pay their pastors. I also know that in some cases churches that have the means to pay their pastors well seem to have made a pact with God saying, "Lord, you keep the pastor humble and we shall keep the pastor poor." Hence, many pastors serve with ongoing sacrifice on the part of their families. I am writing in full recognition of these realities.

Yet, I still assert that one benefit that pastors receive from their churches is being paid for their work, especially their work of pastoral preaching. Such payment is a biblical duty. The Apostle Paul wrote to the Corinthians saying, "Do you not know that those who are employed in the temple service get their food from the temple, and those who serve at the altar share in the sacrificial offerings? In the same way, the Lord commanded that those who proclaim the gospel should get their living by the gospel" (1 Cor 9:13–14).

Earlier, in 1 Corinthians 9:7–11, Paul used argument after argument to show that this command was logical. He asked if the Corinthians knew of any soldier who served for no pay at all. He asked if they knew of anyone who planted a vineyard without eating any of the grapes at harvest time, or any farmer who never drank the milk that the farm animals produced. Paul added Scripture to his argument. He reminded the Corinthians that God commanded the Israelites not to muzzle the oxen that were treading corn on the threshing floor (Deut 25:4). The animals were to be allowed to eat to replenish their energy. Paul then took this physical example and applied it more broadly to the spiritual realm, showing that God's concern was that his people would remunerate all who spent their energies doing spiritual work among them.

When churches pay pastors they are not doing them a favour. They are obeying God. This is one of the benefits of pastoral preaching. As the Apostle Paul said to Timothy, "Let the elders who rule well be considered worthy of double honour, especially those who labour in preaching and teaching. For the Scripture says, 'You shall not muzzle an ox when it treads out the grain,' and, 'The labourer deserves his wages'" (1 Tim 5:17–18). Notice that he undergirds his command to Timothy by quoting the same passage from Deuteronomy and the teachings of Christ. The main reason why pastors should be paid is because they labour in preparing sermons and preaching them. Doing such work well takes a lot of time. So, I repeat, when a church pays the pastor it is not doing the pastor a favour. It is being obedient to God.

The Church Provides Working Teams

All human beings, including pastors, are social creatures. God has not wired us to be isolated trees in the forest of humanity. As an African proverb says, "One finger cannot pick lice." Even in football, it does not matter how talented you are, you still need the other team members in order to win a match. In the same way, those who are involved in pastoral preaching need to work with others. Churches ensure that pastors work in partnership with others rather than in isolation. This allows for sharing of the workload and for mutual accountability.

Fellow elders are the immediate team that the pastor works with. Thus the passage we have just referred to in 1 Timothy 5:17 says, "Let the elders who rule well be considered worthy of double honour, especially those who labour in preaching and teaching." Notice that those who labour in preaching and teaching are doing so in the context of a team of elders. This is because, important as pastoral preaching is in the work of shepherding, it is not the only work. There is also the work of ascertaining the spiritual state of those wanting to join the church, counselling those who are going through difficulties in their Christian lives, leading the various ministries of the church, disciplining erring members, and so on. Elders share these responsibilities so that the pastor can spend most of his energy in pastoral preaching.

Another important role that elders play is that of ensuring mutual accountability. As already stated, it is dangerous for a human being to work alone. We are all fallen creatures. Left to ourselves long enough, we tend to go off on tangents. This is what has led to the fall of many of God's choice servants who work in the context of "one-man ministries." The church provides a context of mutual accountability through eldership boards. Pastors working in a team context pray and work together with their fellow leaders. Any early signs of spiritual deterioration, which are often manifest in preaching, are quickly detected. This is a great benefit for pastors because the devil targets them with his most powerful weapons. He knows that if he can strike the shepherd, he will manage to scatter the sheep.

Then there are others besides the elders who play secondary teaching and diaconal roles. Their responsibilities are important to the overall running of the church but can be energy-draining. Dealing with them would leave the pastor with very little time and energy to pray and prepare for preaching. This is what led to the organizing of the first team of deacons (Acts 6:1–7). The apostles realized that they were spending too much time looking after the widows in the church, and that even so they were not able to give this ministry all the time it needed. In the meantime, their primary work of praying and preaching was suffering. Finally, they asked the church to choose a team that would handle the needs of the widows. The result of this initiative was that the apostles were better able to do their primary work and the church continued to grow.

The Church Provides Good Role Models

One of the most difficult tasks all leaders face is convincing their followers to attempt what they have never done before or to push for heights that they have never reached before. The followers often think that it is impossible. For instance, advocates of conservation farming have had an uphill battle trying to convince rural farmers that they can produce a better crop without resorting to expensive fertilizers. The breakthrough often comes when someone believes enough in conservation farming techniques to give them a try. When that person's farm produces a better crop than neighbouring farms, and when this happens for a few years in succession, the wrong belief is challenged and others begin to give conservation farming a try.

It is the same in the church. Pastoral preaching suffers when there are no mature believers in the church who are living out the principles being advocated from the Bible. I remember listening to a young pastor fresh out of Bible school teaching the men in his church from Ephesians 5:25 about husbands loving their wives. When he told the men that they should tell their wives that they loved them, they burst out laughing. "This young man knows nothing," they said, "That is a Western idea. What will our wives think of us if we start telling them we love them? They will think we have gone crazy!" Not one of the older men in that church was able to stand up and testify that he verbalized his love to his wife. As much as the young pastor tried to show these men that their supreme example was Jesus Christ, who not only loves his church but declares that love again and again in Scripture, he still lost the battle!

It is not until some believers in the church reach spiritual maturity and begin to make a break from their cultural norms in response to the demands of Scripture that progress suddenly begins to be seen. Thankfully, it is often only a matter of time because spiritual growth is inevitable where souls are truly regenerate. Once this begins to happen and younger believers begin to see older believers living out the kind of lives being advocated in the preaching, the excuses are reduced and the pastor begins to see more believers responding speedily to what is being preaching. This great benefit to the pastor's work is not always very obvious to those who are watching from the outside.

In the wisdom of God, he has given pastors a very good working environment, which exceeds even that of the lawyer, the doctor, the carpenter, or the chief. Where the church is already healthy, pastoral preaching can be a real joy. But where the church is stubborn and the people are disaffected, pastoral preaching can also be a heartache. Sadly, there are even pastors who have been forced to resign from their positions.

So we must never underestimate the role of the church in ensuring the success of our work. In fact, every pastor should be grateful to God for the church. Yes, the church benefits from pastoral preaching, but pastoral preaching also benefits from the church

Discussion Questions

1. What was your experience as you were preparing for pastoral ministry? How did your pastor nurture you for the work you are now doing?

2. If someone told you that they sensed a call to pastoral ministry, what questions would you ask them that would show the relevance of the church in their call?

3. What practical advice would you give to a rural church to help them grow in their sense of responsibility for the remuneration of their pastor?

4. Have you experienced other benefits of being a pastor preaching in the context of the local church that are not listed in this chapter?

5

Pastoral Preaching Benefits the Church

When I was in secondary school, our biology teacher taught us a big word – symbiosis. I had never heard the word before. He explained, "Symbiosis is when two organisms depend on each other for their sustenance." He said that we all have bacteria in our stomachs and intestines that help us to break down the food that we eat so that it can be absorbed by our bodies. He also explained that the bacteria survive by living within us and would perish if they were expelled from our bodies. That is a mutually beneficial relationship. Forty years later, I still remember the lesson!

That lesson came alive again as I thought about the relationship between pastoral preaching and the church. It is a symbiotic relationship, a mutually beneficial relationship. The church benefits from pastoral preaching and pastoral preaching benefits from the church. In the last chapter, we saw how pastoral preaching benefits from the church. Now, I want us to see the various ways in which the church benefits from pastoral preaching.

It Gives the Church a Sense of God

In his famous book on preaching entitled *Preaching and Preachers*, Dr Martyn Lloyd-Jones wrote, "What is the chief end of preaching? I like to think it is this. It is to give men and women a sense of God and His presence."[1] This is the first benefit that pastoral preaching gives to the church – a sense of God.

The Apostle Paul referred to this sense of God when he spoke of prophecy in the New Testament: "But if all prophesy, and an unbeliever or outsider

---

1. D. Martyn Lloyd-Jones and Bryan Chapell, *Preaching and Preachers* (Reprint, Grand Rapids: Zondervan, 2011), 97.

enters, he is convicted by all, he is called to account by all, the secrets of his heart are disclosed, and so, falling on his face, he will worship God and declare that God is really among you" (1 Cor 14:24–25). That is what all preaching should do. It should convict those who listen to it and cause them to sense that they are accountable to God. They should realize that their lives are fully exposed before this God. Preaching should leave the listeners worshipping God in his very presence.

Men and women come to church with a lot of mundane things on their minds. Life is not easy. Unemployment is high. AIDS is reaping its thousands on every side. Islamic terrorist groups are wreaking havoc. Young people are worried about their future. These are the types of thoughts that are occupying many minds, and they can be quite overwhelming to the point of obscuring the reality of God in life. When people come to church, they need to be redirected to see that God is real and that he is concerned about the smallest details of their lives. This is what preaching does. It causes men and women to be conscious that beyond the physical reality there is the spiritual presence of God, who is in control of all things.

"Thus saith the Lord" (to use an old phrase from the King James Version of the Bible) is often a wake-up call to people who have been hearing all sorts of other voices all week. Movies, politicians, and sports and music personalities have occupied the airwaves, giving their opinions about life. These voices tend to shape popular thinking, often in ways that go against the mind of God. When worshippers go to church they are confronted with "Thus saith the Lord" and all those false notions are smoked out of their minds – at least to some extent.

This sense of God is not produced by the preacher being louder than the politician or the popular personality. It is produced by the presence of the Holy Spirit who attends the faithful preaching of the Word of God. He is the one who convicts the hearers, bringing awareness that the all-seeing eye of God is upon them and making them sense that God is having dealings with them in the here and now as they listen to the preaching of his Word.

It Enables the Church to Face Its Corporate Sins

In our private or family Bible readings, the Word of God speaks to us as individuals and as families. A lot of benefit comes to us through that, and so we need to thank God that the Bible is available for us as individuals and families to read in our own time. However, there is an added advantage when the Bible is expounded in the gathered church. It speaks to us collectively as God's people and shows us the corporate sins we need to repent of.

Think, for example, of the divisions between Jews and Gentiles in the early church and of the abuse of the Lord's Supper in the church in Corinth. These were corporate sins, and the Apostle Paul wrote to the churches to deal with them. If he had been there in person, he would have preached on these subjects so that the churches would understand God's mind about what was going on. That is what pastoral preaching is supposed to achieve in the church.

An obvious example I can give in the current African situation is syncretism. The tendency in many churches is to combine Christianity with practices drawn from African traditional religion. There is even a saying; "Charms are more powerful when they are mixed with God." Hence, you find church elders visiting witch doctors to seek protection from evil spirits and then coming to church to worship God – and the church accepts this as normal. The faithful preaching of the Word of God in a pastoral context should show the self-contradictory nature of such behaviour until the church collectively senses a need to deal with the matter and make the necessary reforms.

Corporate sins are often cultural, and so they are blind spots that we are not conscious of until the Word of God is carefully and consistently taught and applied in that area. That is one reason why they are best addressed at a corporate level. Polygamy is one such example. It is so embedded in the fabric of some parts of rural and urban Africa that even after people are converted they do not immediately see the error of having more than one wife. Everyone is doing it. It is a societal norm . . . until pastoral preaching begins to show God's blueprint for marriage. Then questions begin to be raised in the church, enabling it to come up with a biblical policy towards marriage as God intended it to be.

It Gives Worship Services a Great Crescendo

A worship service is incomplete without the preaching of the Word of God. When the people of God meet together to worship God, two-way communication takes place. They bring to God their prayers, their singing, and their financial substance (to support God's work) and, in return, God speaks to them through his Word. It is primarily through preaching that God communicates with the people. So pastoral preaching fulfils people's expectation of meeting with God in the worship service.

In fact, pastoral preaching gives the worship services a great crescendo and sends the worshippers home with a glorious sense of satisfaction. This is largely because they have sensed God's presence and recognized areas of life that need to be reformed in obedience to God.

Imagine the situation described by the Apostle Paul in 1 Corinthians 14, of an unbeliever who visits a worship service and finally exclaims, "God is really among you." He probably came to church quite indifferent to spiritual things and caring very little about cleaning up his life in a moral and spiritual sense. He probably came fully engrossed with his own little world and simply wanting to pass some time or to meet some friends. However, as the preaching started, he was gripped by a power he had not experienced before. His thoughts were laid bare before him. He saw his guilt before God and in the end he sought the Saviour. What a glorious end to his church visit.

Many years ago, when I was still a university student and more in the pew than in the pulpit, I recall going back to university at the end of worship services feeling as if I had just gone through the most exhilarating experience in the whole universe. What made me feel like this was often the great preaching I had heard. It made me look forward to the next Lord's Day because this experience was so different from the dry lectures I had to endure all week at the university. The two were poles apart.

The joy that comes from hearing the Word should not only be felt on the individual level but should be shared by the whole church as they sit under pastoral preaching on a weekly basis. They should sense that this is the climax of their worship as God, as it were, comes down and speaks to them through his Word. This joy should be evident as they walk home together through the village or talk among themselves around a meal at home. They may refer to a song or two that they sang, but most of their conversation should be like that of the disciples of Christ on the road to Emmaus in Luke 24:32: "Did not our hearts burn within us . . . while he opened to us the Scriptures?"

It Gives the Church Unity in Doctrine

Pastoral preaching gives the church as a body a growing sense of unity in their doctrinal understanding. The church comprises people from diverse backgrounds. Some come from traditional religions and have as much knowledge of biblical doctrine as a village goat. Others have grown up in church. Still others come from a context that has a doctrinal mixture of the good, the bad, and the ugly. When all these people become members of the same church, their belief systems need to be unified. Otherwise there will be friction and misunderstanding, which may even result in a church split. We often say, "Birds of a feather flock together." Pastoral preaching helps believers to become birds of a feather.

As all these individuals from diverse backgrounds sit under pastoral preaching they begin to wrestle with common truths and start seeing things in a similar way. This is because of the focus areas of pastoral preaching that we covered earlier. Remember that we said pastoral preaching gives those who sit under it (1) a comprehensive view of the gospel, (2) a working knowledge of the Bible, and (3) an appreciation of sound doctrine. The result will be a church that has a common understanding of Christian doctrine.

The Apostle Paul spoke of this unity when he wrote, "He gave the apostles, the prophets, the evangelists, the shepherds and teachers, to equip the saints for the work of ministry, for building up the body of Christ, *until we all attain to the unity of the faith and of the knowledge of the Son of God*, to mature manhood, to the measure of the stature of the fullness of Christ" (Eph 4:11–13, emphasis mine). Nothing can be clearer than that.

Since the church is "a pillar and buttress of the truth" (1 Tim 3:15), it is vital that its members have a common understanding of what that truth is, as far as is humanly possible. The world ought to be guided by the church as to its understanding of who God is, how he saves lost humanity, and what his demands are upon us as his moral creatures. That is only possible if the church itself is unified in its understanding of those truths.

Since new members are constantly being added to the church and the world is never short of false teachings – both old and new – the church will always be in need of pastoral preaching to weed out wrong beliefs and establish it collectively in sound doctrine. Sadly, there are some pastors who think that doctrine divides and so they avoid making clear doctrinal statements in their preaching. They prefer to major in what they call "practical sermons" on how to love one another and look after God's world. But when a new cult comes into town, such churches tend to lose a number of members, often after a period of internal doctrinal strife. These churches are not inoculated against error because the people have not been helped to come to a united understanding of Christian doctrine.

It Gives the Church Stability in Storms

Every so often, the Lord allows his people to endure unique and painful storms. It is like a repetition of what Jesus told Peter when he said, "Simon, Simon, behold, Satan demanded to have you, that he might sift you like wheat" (Luke 22:31). Jesus was referring to the time when he was going to be taken away from his disciples through his arrest, trial, and crucifixion. It was going to be a very difficult time for them. Judas would betray Jesus and later commit suicide, and Peter himself would deny the Lord no less than three times. It was going to be a period of sifting.

Churches also have their times of sifting. God allows them to pass through storms. The trials could be of a physical nature, such as the illness and death of a leader or someone who was in the prime of life, oppression by political leaders or Islamic extremists, and so on. The trials could also be of a spiritual nature, such as the backsliding of a leader in the church resulting in a public scandal and a backlash against the church in the community. Such situations cause much soul-searching on the part of believers. The weak tend to fall away, at least for a season.

Pastoral preaching helps to provide stability to the church during such times. It gives believers a biblical perspective on the situation so that they are not overly alarmed and do not fall into despair. They understand that such trials are meant to test their faith as through fire and that when they come out on the opposite end, they will be purer than gold.

Jesus helped his disciples in a similar fashion on the eve of his crucifixion. He knew that he would soon depart from them in a very traumatic way, and so he spent many hours with them preparing them for the storm. He said, "I have said all these things to you to keep you from falling away. They will put you out of the synagogues. Indeed, the hour is coming when whoever kills you will think he is offering service to God . . . But I have said these things to you, that when their hour comes you may remember that I told them to you" (John 16:1–4). The teaching would help them to process the persecution when it finally came.

That is what pastoral preaching does. After years of being fed a biblically balanced diet, believers know that there will be storms in this world. However, the same teaching had led them to know that Jesus has overcome the world (John 16:33). So when the storms hit, the teachings they have received over the years will act like ballast in a boat, giving it stability as the waves pound it and the wind howls in the rigging. This is a real benefit that the church derives from pastoral preaching.

It is also important that during a season of trial (for instance, when a member of the church dies), pastors take a break from any series of teachings they are giving in order to preach a message that is relevant to the circumstances. That is what true shepherding is all about. It responds to the immediate situation the sheep are passing through. The church may be going through a period of mourning or discouragement. It is vital that God's Word be allowed to comfort and encourage his people. The pastor must strike while the iron is still hot. The consciences of God's people are very tender at such a time and their minds are sober, and so they are likely to get maximum benefit from the preached Word. Once that difficult season is over, the pastor may return to the series of teachings that was interrupted so that consistency of teaching is maintained.

It Causes Church Growth by Attracting Older Believers

One of the most significant ways in which a church grows is through its evangelistic efforts. New believers, fresh out of the world, come into the church through baptism. This is by far the best form of church growth because it is adding to the numbers in the kingdom of God. However, there is another way in which a church grows and it is through the movement of believers from one place to another. Often these movements occur when people get new jobs or retire and consequently have to relocate. As they get into the new area, one of their immediate goals is to find "a good church." What criteria do they use to find one?

A major deciding factor is the quality of the preaching. They want to settle down in a church where they are assured that they will grow spiritually and so look for a church with a good pulpit ministry. Older believers who are moving into the area may even be even willing to travel a fair distance to get to the church. A church grows by adding older believers as well as new believers when it has a good pulpit ministry.

Pastoral preaching attracts older believers not only because it promises them a good spiritual diet but also because it sets the spiritual atmosphere of the church as a whole. Mature believers often take their time to settle on a new church because they want their family to enjoy a wholesome spiritual ambience. They do their homework well. In addition to listening to the sermons, their antennas are normally picking up signals about the church's health in general. Good pastoral preaching often results in a healthy body of believers with wholesome church dynamics. Older believers pick up very quickly and they want to be a part of it. Thus they soon express an interest in joining such a church.

Sadly, the opposite is equally true. A church that has not benefitted from good pastoral preaching for a meaningful length of time is one that tends to be full of strife. I recall visiting a Christian many years ago who told me that some people were asking him to join a particular church so that he could "help them sort out their pastor." That message was enough to keep him away from that church! He was mature enough to know that if you join a fight whose origin you were never a part of, you will simply add to the confusion. Mature believers want to join a church that is peaceful and steadily growing.

Growth through older believers has its benefits. They are already mature in doctrinal understanding and godly habits. They come with the wealth of experience they have garnered over the years through their walk with God. In Bible discussions, their input is invaluable and goes a long way to augmenting the teaching of the pastor. Younger believers are given instant examples of what spiritual maturity looks like. Older believers are already "cooked" and ready to be "served." The church can immediately put them to work as teachers and leaders in the various departments of the church. Some of them may soon become elders and deacons in the church.

It Gives the Church a Sense of Purpose

Finally, pastoral preaching gives a church a sense of purpose so that the army of God can work together to accomplish the purpose for which Christ instituted it. This is important because without a sense of purpose people tend to feel frustrated. They have energy but they do not know how or where to use it. They are all going in different directions and end up stepping on each other's toes. That is neither good for them nor for their collective existence.

The church's agenda goes beyond its weekly meetings on the Lord's Day. Jesus commanded the church to disciple all the nations (Matt 28:16–20). These marching orders remain relevant in every generation and wherever the church is planted. Accomplishing this task will demand the use of all the church's resources in terms of manpower and money.

As God's people sit under pastoral preaching, they are informed about the church's work and the urgency of its mandate so that they throw in their weight behind this work. The Great Commission is echoed again and again in the preaching, and relaxing in the background is no longer seen as an option. Recognizing their various gifts, individuals in the church begin to see how they can join hands with other believers to proclaim the crown-rights of King Jesus to the four corners of the earth.

In addition to the outward purpose of reaching the world, there is also the purpose of fulfilling the inward life of the church. The church senses that it ought to be a family of love, taking care of God's individual precious children. As God gives his children blessings, they sense that this is not incidental. God wants them to share these blessings with other believers in order to lighten their burdens as they travel together to heaven. Pastoral preaching teaches believers that "religion that is pure and undefiled before God, the Father, is this: to visit orphans and widows in their affliction, and to keep oneself unstained from the world" (Jas 1:27). This makes the church a loving community.

So, the church as a corporate body stands to benefit a lot from pastoral preaching. The relationship between the church and the pastor who exercises a regular preaching ministry within its context is a symbiotic one! Both stand to benefit from the relationship. Where this relationship is healthy, the pastor's gifts will be exercised to the glory of God while the church will grow until it fulfils its purpose in a God-honouring way. That is how God intended it to be. In the next chapter, we will consider the implications of all this for both the church and the pastor.

Discussion Questions

1. In what other ways apart from conviction of sin do people experience "the sense of God" during the preaching of the Word of God?

2. If God's people enjoy other aspects of the worship services more than the preaching, what should a pastor do to make preaching a great climax for them?

3. What are some of the corporate sins of the church in your culture that pastoral preaching can and should be addressing?

4. Have there been any storms in your church or in a church that you know of? How did pastoral preaching help the church to come out of the storm?

6

Implications of the Church-Pastor Relationship

It is evident from the last two chapters that there is a reciprocal relationship between pastoral preaching and the church. Good pastoral preaching grows a good and healthy church, which in turn provides a good environment for good pastoral preaching. The opposite is equally true. Poor pastoral preaching soon produces a spiritually unhealthy church, which in turn becomes antagonistic to good preaching. So, the relationship between pastoral preaching and the local church is never static. It springs upwards or spirals downwards.

Any visiting preacher can tell when he is preaching in a church that is privileged to have a good pulpit ministry. The congregation is like a sponge, sucking in the words as they are preached from the pulpit. Similarly, a visiting preacher can tell when he is preaching in a church with a poor pulpit ministry. There it is hard to get the people's attention, they are always fidgeting, and there is hardly any connection and concentration.

In this chapter, let us look at what needs to be done to ensure that we maximize the church-pastor relationship.

Implications for the Pastor

The pastor's relationship to the people of God imposes clear obligations.

Love the People of God

Pastoral preaching should flow out of a heart that dearly loves the people of God in the church. This love first manifests itself in a pastor's desire to know the individuals and families in the church and the circumstances in which they live. As pastors we will want to know the trials and temptations that our people are going through so that we can minister to them appropriately through the Word of God. Love will compel us to get involved in the lives of the people of God and develop relationships even with their children. We will seek to know the names of the parents and their children so that we can pray for them by name. Love will drive us to our knees to pray for the flock.

The Apostle Paul warned, "If I speak in the tongues of men and of angels, but have not love, I am a noisy gong or a clanging cymbal" (1 Cor 13:1). How true that is! God's people can usually tell whether pastors are simply filling in the allotted time in the pulpit or whether they are seeking to reach their hearers' hearts because they love them deeply. When love is missing, preaching is nothing but a repetitive, irritating noise. When there is love, the pulpit is like a fire around which the whole village gathers at night to keep warm while they listen to the stories and wisdom of the village elders.

When the Apostle Paul wrote to the Christians in Philippi, this is how he spoke to them: "Therefore, my brothers, whom I love and long for, my joy and crown, stand firm thus in the Lord, my beloved" (Phil 4:1). The church in Philippi was the first that Paul had planted in Europe. He had been their pastor until the Holy Spirit sent him further into Europe to plant more churches. It is evident that his love for them ran deep, because many years later he still refers to them as brothers whom he loves and longs for. He still calls them "my beloved." That is the heart of a true pastor. He loves the people of God whom he shepherds through the ministry of the Word. As a pastor, this must be true of you.

It is this love that made the Apostle Paul write, "And, apart from other things, there is the daily pressure on me of my anxiety for all the churches. Who is weak, and I am not weak? Who is made to fall, and I am not indignant?" (2 Cor 11:28–29). Love drove him to write the magnificent letters that make up most of the New Testament. Love propelled him to communicate relevant divine truths to churches that were struggling with sin and error. He wanted to see healthy churches. That is how it is with true pastors. The condition of the people of God causes us sleepless nights. It is in those dark hours of the night as we wrestle with God that sermons are born that will impact God's people forever.

Having said that, I must hurry to state that a pastor must balance the time spent visiting the flock and the time spent in sermon preparation. We all have our biases. Some pastors are so sociable that being alone preparing sermons is like torture. They want to be "out there." However, this begins to show in the watery sermons that they preach, and soon the congregation will be complaining about the poor sermons to which they are being subjected. So, ensure that part of your love for God's people glues you to your chair as you prepare three-course spiritual meals for them.

Pass on Christian Truth

In a previous chapter we looked at the focus of pastoral preaching. The point I made there is so important that it is worth repeating here, for it has important implications for the pastor-church relationship. It is stated in the book of Acts that the first New Testament church committed itself to the apostles' teaching (Acts 2:42). Timothy was told to preach the Word, which was "profitable for teaching, for reproof, for correction, and for training in righteousness" (2 Tim 3:16). In both these verses, the word "teaching" was translated "doctrine" in older versions of the Bible, because what is being spoken of here is the body of truth that makes up the Christian faith. That is what the apostles were passing on to the early church. That is what makes the Holy Scriptures so useful. A pastor is able to pass on Christian truth by teaching from the Bible.

Sadly, too many sermons in the church in Africa today do not ground the people of God in the truths of the Christian faith. Rather, as stated in the previous chapter, we tend to major in "practical" or "how to" sermons based purely on what the Apostle Paul calls "philosophy and empty deceit, according to human tradition, according to the elementary spirits of the world, and not according to Christ" (Col 2:8). Such sermons are very attractive to the natural mind because they talk about how to be successful, how to be victorious, how to be happily married, and so on. Who does not want that? Yet they fail to deliver on their promises because they lack the truth according to Christ. Those who preach them are yielding to today's consumer mentality. Like supermarkets, they are trying to give people what they want. So their sermons are designed to attract people and fill the pews. In the end, such pastors have the numbers but not the spirituality.

Those of us who are pastors are called to pass on the Christian faith to those whom we shepherd week after week. From our pulpit ministry, they must learn to know the true God who has revealed himself in creation and in the Bible. They must be helped to know this God in all his attributes, and not only hear about those attributes that appeal to human selfishness. Then they will want to live for the glory of God alone. The people of God must also know the true human condition before and after the fall, as recorded in Genesis, so that they can understand why human beings do the atrocious things they do. Their understanding of human nature must issue into a clear knowledge of how God saves from sin through the work of his Son, Jesus Christ, and through the work of the Holy Spirit.

In the chapter that dealt with the focus of pastoral preaching, we saw that pastors must help Christians develop a working knowledge of the Bible and an appreciation of sound doctrine. Through the pulpit ministry, the people of God should come to appreciate the nature of true godliness and the fight of faith so that they can live in a way that glorifies God. Those are the big issues that pastoral preaching should concentrate on. We owe it to the church to ensure believers are well taught, so that when our time comes to an end, we will leave churches that are healthy and strong, not churches that are skewed towards our particular hobbyhorse.

Implications for the Church

Having looked at the implications of the church-pastor relationship for the pastor, let us now turn to its implications for the church.

Give Priority to the Preacher

The first point that needs to be made is that the church needs to treasure the elders who have a preaching role. Whenever I deal with this matter I must quickly state again that I recognize that there are various forms of church government. My aim is not to enter into debate about which form is the biblical one. Rather, in the light of how the fortunes of the church are tied up with the pulpit ministry, I want to argue for giving priority to the preaching gifts in the church's leadership structure and in its work of extending the kingdom of God.

In too many churches, there is a view that all church leaders or elders must be given an equal opportunity to participate in pastoral preaching. In other churches, as long as you are male and have been in the church long enough for people to know you, you must also be given space in the teaching ministry of the church. This is an overreaction to what is perceived as one-man ministry. This approach fails to see that the Lord Jesus Christ gives different gifts to different people in his church, and one of these gifts is the gift of preaching and teaching "to equip the saints for the work of ministry, for building up the body of Christ" (Eph 4:11). Let us admit it; not everyone – and not even every elder – has the gift of preaching.

The problem is even worse in rural churches where the term "elder" is often confused with "elderly." Since the teaching role in the village is left to the aged, the same philosophy is applied in the church. Instead of giving priority to those who are gifted in preaching and teaching, the tendency is to give this responsibility to those who exercise this role in the community at large. When they are around, the pulpit is handed over to them. In places where education levels are very poor, the pulpit may be quickly handed over to unregenerate but educated men from the city simply because they can read the Bible. Again, this is a failure to see that the church operates under a different philosophy from the world. Jesus, the head of the church, has given it preachers and teachers. They must be given room to do their work.

The preaching and teaching ministry of pastors also suggests that they should be the ones to provide leadership among the elders of the church. I was once invited to hold a week of evangelistic meetings in a church that had a history of changing pastors in quick succession. Because of these frequent changes in leadership, the church remained anaemic and small for a very long time while other churches around it were thriving. For the whole week I was there I did not realize that the church actually had a pastor. There was an elder who was evidently in charge. He was conspicuously the wealthiest person in the congregation and had a very high position in the government. He was the one who had written to invite me to preach there. He welcomed me to the meetings and he introduced me to the congregation. On the final day, a man came to greet me and almost apologetically introduced himself as the church's pastor. While I was trying to acquaint myself with him, the elder arrived and began to instruct the pastor about the protocol to be observed as they closed the final meeting: the elder would call the pastor to bring him the gift, and then he would present the gift to me before closing in prayer. "Yes sir" the pastor replied, almost sheepishly. Not surprisingly, a few months later I was told that pastor too had resigned!

It is almost impossible to exercise true pastoral preaching in a church where you have an elder who will not let you provide overall leadership. As a pastor you feel suffocated because you are expected to simply echo someone else's voice. This is why it is often suggested that a former pastor should leave the church for a considerable length of time to enable his successor to become the leader as well as the pastoral preacher. The importance of the pastor's stepping into this role cannot be overemphasized.

Guard the Time for Preaching

When the New Testament was being written, there were many extraordinary gifts in the church and they were all competing for prominence when the church gathered. The Apostle Paul was concerned that spectacular gifts were being given greater priority than the gifts of preaching and teaching, and so he advised that the gift of prophecy should be given priority over the gift of tongues: "The one who prophesies is greater than the one who speaks in tongues, unless someone interprets, so that the church may be built up" (1 Cor 14:5). The gathered church is a place for vital education and so it is important for time to be preserved for pastoral preaching.

I have already alluded to Acts 2:42 where it is stated that the early church was devoted to the apostles' teaching. This meant that the Christians spent a lot of time learning from the apostles. This was a priority in their lives. They did not allow the other demands of life and living to crowd out the time for learning from the apostles. That is what devotion means. It means giving something top priority even when there are other pressures.

Churches should have set times for teaching the people of God. Often, this will be on the Lord's Day. However, many churches also have another day in the week when believers come together for prayer and instruction from the Word of God. While it is the responsibility of pastors to ensure that they are well prepared to teach on all the occasions set apart for the instruction of the flock, it is also the responsibility of church members to ensure that they are present for such sessions. Christians must commit themselves to attending the sessions of instruction in their local church. That is the only way they will grow.

Sadly, this is often not the case in our day. Christians skip church services and Bible studies at every excuse. The young professionals in the churches are constantly chasing higher pay cheques and promotions, which often means working long hours and even going to the office on the Lord's Day. Young families fill their diaries with so many activities related to their children's recreation that there is very little time for them to spend under the instruction of their pastors. In the West many churches close down most of their teaching programmes in the summer because church folk tend to go away on vacation, and in rural Africa churches do the same during planting and harvest times when church folk spend seven days a week working on their farms. In both cases, the needs of the body take precedence over the needs of the soul. Sometimes these needs are legitimate because Christians are not disembodied spirits. However, where it is clear that church services and Bible studies are being skipped at every excuse, this imbalance needs to be sensitively addressed so that biblical priorities are restored.

Another competitor to the preaching and teaching time in worship services is the amount of singing that takes place in most of our churches. I recall preaching at a church where various choirs sang – the men's choir, the women's choir, the youth choir, the children's choir, the quartet, the soloist, and so on. By the time I was called upon to preach, I could tell that everyone was ready to go home. I was asked to preach for no more than twenty minutes in a service that lasted no less than three hours!

If this were the exception, I would not be addressing the matter here. However, what happened then is, sadly, only a slight exaggerated form of what happens in many African churches. We need to jealously guard the time given to pastoral preaching and not allow it to be crowded out by our love of singing. Let us remember that the early church was characterized by devotion to the apostles' teaching. This partly explains why the church became a force to reckon with in its own day.

If there were rich doctrinal content in most of our songs, I might not be so opposed to spending a long time in singing. Many songs that we inherited from the missionaries who came to establish the church in Africa are rich with doctrinal truths. They are a form of instruction in themselves. However, never-ending choruses that repeat empty phrases have replaced most of these rich hymns. Often the songs vaguely celebrate a benevolent divine being who continues to bless us, taking us from here to there and enabling us to make progress in life. The words of these songs are not necessarily untrue, but they are a very poor substitute for the kind of pastoral preaching I am advocating in this book. The time given to them needs to be reduced.

Support the Pastor Financially

Finally, I come to money matters. If the church is to truly benefit from the church-pastor relationship, there needs to be concerted effort to ensure that pastors are fully financially supported by the church. Bi-vocational pastors can give only a little of their time to the work of pastoral preaching. By the time they leave their secular workplace, they may have only enough energy to crawl into bed and sleep. Where will they find the time and energy to prepare biblically rich and relevant sermons that will build a people for God? This matter needs serious attention if the church is not to remain weak.

Many churches in Africa are also still recovering from a foreign missionary hangover. When those missionaries were planting churches and doing other missionary work, they were not affected by the church's poor financial giving because their support came from overseas. Even if the Christians never tithed, the church's programmes were not affected. Most of the church buildings were constructed using foreign funds. This benevolence from abroad has crippled the African church to the point that even in cities where churches are bursting at the seams with professionals, the giving is meagre. It is a pale reflection of the earning power of the congregants.

A herculean effort needs to be made to reverse this attitude. I have already referred to churches that give the impression that they have entered into covenant with God, saying, "Lord, keep your servants humble and we will keep them poor." This needs to change, especially in the light of biblical injunctions. Remember the Apostle Paul's words, "Let the elders who rule well be considered worthy of double honour, especially those who labour in preaching and teaching. For the Scripture says, 'You shall not muzzle an ox when it treads out the grain,' and 'The labourer deserves his wages'" (1 Tim 5:17–18). Providing financial support for pastors is not an optional extra. The health of any church depends on the quality of the ongoing preaching ministry. So churches must make it a high priority not only to have good pastors preaching to them but also to pay their pastors well enough for them to be able to care for their own families' needs.

There are two excuses normally given in our African context. The first is poverty. We never seem to have enough to feed our own families, so how can we spare anything to support the person who pastors the church and leads church ministries? The biblical injunction is "let the one who is taught the word share all good things with the one who teaches" (Gal 6:6). In other words, all God is asking is that you share what you have with the one who feeds you God's Word. Surely, even in your poverty you have something. Share it!

The second excuse is taxation. The government has already taxed us. Why should the church also tax us? If that is your attitude towards your tithes and offerings, then it is best that you do not give to the Lord's work because God loves a cheerful giver. The Bible says, "Each one must give as he has decided in his heart, not reluctantly or under compulsion, for God loves a cheerful giver" (2 Cor 9:7). The point that the government is making when it taxes us is that nothing is free. If you expect people to govern and serve you and maintain your roads and your surroundings, you need to pay for their services. The government taxes you and pays those who are serving you in this way. Well, surely, the church is doing much the same thing. Pastors do not walk into shops and get free groceries for their children. They pay for those commodities. Where will they get the money to do that? It must be from the people whom they serve. So, if we want our pastors to serve us well, we need to pay them well.

Remember the word "symbiosis." The pastor benefits from the church and the church benefits from the pastor. A healthy relationship between the two will result in a great pastoral preaching experience and an effective and growing church. It is up to the church and the pastor to make this happen by ensuring that we are all doing our part in this relationship. It is like a marriage. If each person concentrates only on what he or she is supposed to get out of the relationship, the couple will soon end up at the *induna's* court asking for a divorce. However, if they both concentrate on what they are supposed to put into the relationship, their marriage will be the envy of the whole village or township because it will be a little heaven on earth. So, concentrate on your part in this symbiotic relationship and see what God will do in your church.

Discussion Questions

1. How can you as a pastor grow in your love for the people in your church, including those who have very difficult characters?

2. What practical steps can you take to structure your worship service so that the preaching of the Word has its rightful place?

3. Is there anything that you can do to help your members prioritize attending the educational meetings of the church?

4. What counsel would you give to a new pastor who is being frustrated by a very strong leader who will not yield to his leadership?

Section C

How We Train for Pastoral Preaching

7

Pastors Model Pastoral Preaching

As I write this book, I have been pastoring Kabwata Baptist Church for almost thirty years. For about half of that period I worked without formal training, for I had never been to Bible school. Yet I knew what I had to do, and my pastoral preaching met with some measure of success. Mine is not an unusual story. My two closest friends in the pastoral ministry also began their pastoral work before receiving any formal training, and they have had very distinguished pastoral careers. Two of the most respected preachers in the last 150 years, Charles Haddon Spurgeon and Martyn Lloyd-Jones, had no formal theological training. In Africa, due to the paucity of Bible colleges compared to the rate of growth of the Christian church, very few pastors receive formal training before embarking upon their work. This is especially true in rural Africa.

I highlight all this not because I despise formal theological training but because I want us to recognize that there is another form of training that takes place in the lives of most future pastors long before they enter Bible college. This is the informal training they receive from the pastors under whose ministries they sit. In an earlier chapter I referred to this as one of the benefits pastors get from churches. Pastoral preaching is caught before it is taught.

I was converted in 1979 and spent the next five years sitting under the ministry of Pastor Joe Simfukwe at Lusaka Baptist Church. In those five years I occupied the front pew almost every Sunday and soaked up his preaching like a sponge. Little did I know that I was learning not only the content of pastoral preaching but also the "how to" of pastoral preaching. After surviving the first ten years of being a pastor, I wrote to my former pastor and thanked him for his example. I told him that he had been my role model and that everything good in my preaching thus far was a result of what I had learnt from him.

What are some of the lessons one learns from a serving pastor that a Bible college cannot teach?

Balancing Sermon Preparation with Other Duties

The first lesson I want to highlight is simply that pastors have to prepare good sermons despite their other demanding responsibilities. A busy pastorate is no excuse for poor sermons. During the week, a pastor should be busy with visitation, conducting funerals, comforting the sick, counselling the troubled, and leading various church meetings and ministries. Then on Sunday that same pastor should hear a sermon of such quality that the congregation that a whole week must have been devoted to nothing else but preparing it. They should start to wonder how on earth their pastor manages to do this.

By observing a pastor at work, the future pastor learns that sermon preparation is not an excuse for not visiting the flock and providing good leadership to the church. The two areas of work must go together in a healthy balance. A pastor must have a hidden life that is spent working hard to prepare good sermons as well as a public life devoted to other pastoral duties. That is how you build a people for God.

Church members may get a glimpse into the hidden work of sermon preparation when they visit the pastor for pastoral counselling. They may find the pastor in an office or study with an open Bible and other books and papers on the desk. There will be some pages of handwritten notes (though these days in urban areas these notes are more likely to be on the computer screen). The pastor may look up when they arrive and say something like, "Welcome. You have found me in the midst of my sermon preparation, but this is a good time to take a break." And so, the church members discover that their pastor does not pluck good sermons out of the air but needs to have time away from the hectic public demands to prepare them.

I speak from experience. My first visit to my pastor in his study left a deep impression on me. I remember thinking, "So *this* is where those powerful sermons come from!" My pastor's study was not the usual African pastor's study because he had been trained in the United Kingdom and had come back with quite a sizeable library. All four walls of his study were lined with books, and his desk was laden with the books he was using that day. I could tell from the titles of some of those books that they were relevant to the current series of messages he was preaching. His table was also cluttered with papers. I had finally entered the man's secret chamber. It was awesome!

Preaching Sermons That Grip Hearers

Another lesson a future pastor learns while sitting under the ministry of a serving pastor is how to preach sermons that transfix hearers. This is not something that can be learnt in a classroom situation; you have to see it happening. It is not even something you learn from roving evangelists because they tend to have a few powerful sermons that they repeat wherever they go. To have a successful pastorate you need to produce powerful sermons for the same congregation week after week, for many years. This cannot be stage-managed.

Let me take you back to my formative years at Lusaka Baptist Church under the ministry of Pastor Joe Simfukwe. His sermons were not full of flowery language and rhetorical flourishes. He simply wanted to communicate what a particular passage of Scripture was saying to us today. Yet, there were many Sundays when he preached me out of my socks, and many of my friends would testify of the same.

There is very little restlessness in the congregation while such a sermon is being preached. I remember that there was a slightly squeaky fan in the church in Lusaka. When the pastor reached the height of his sermon, there was such complete silence that you could even hear the soft squeak of that fan. The Lord was speaking to his people through his servant.

Another way in which you can tell that a sermon has gripped people is their surprise when it ends. They look at their watches, thinking that the service has ended early, only to discover that it was the usual length. They are left wanting more. They are eager for the next opportunity to learn from their pastor. The ability to preach such sermons cannot be taught in Bible college. It must be experienced in the life of the church.

I sat under that kind of preaching for the first five years of my Christian life. There were no gimmicks, and yet our attention was riveted on what was being said. Like the disciples on the road to Emmaus in Luke 24:32, we often said, "Did not our hearts burn within us while he talked to us . . . while he opened to us the Scriptures?" I remember praying, "Lord, if you ever open a door for me to enter into pastoral work, I want to preach like that!"

Not every preacher has gripped me with his preaching. I have listened to preachers who have said everything they had to say in the first five minutes and spent the rest of the time going around in circles wasting everyone's time. Some of them had good content, but either the material was not in good logical order or the preacher simply failed to hook the attention of the congregation and so everyone was restless. I do not want to be that kind of preacher.

Preaching Sermons That Build Believers and Churches

Many people want to attend churches where the preacher is witty and full of jokes and anecdotes. There the sermons do not them uncomfortable, even if they have been living in sin all week. But while such preaching can draw crowds, it does not necessarily build a people for God. Such congregations tend to be spiritually weak and self-centred, and such churches are rocked by all kinds of scandals even in their top leadership.

The young and impressionable are easily taken in by such pastors. But we need to remember that it is one thing to hear a good sermon and sense its impact on you and on others. It is another to see over a period of time the kind of preaching that actually builds believers and churches. The former is spectacular but the latter is where true spiritual health comes from. It is the type of preaching that creates the type of church that mature believers want to join. Someone who wants to be used by God to build good strong churches should follow the example of preaching that impacts people over the long haul. This is yet another lesson that one learns best by first-hand experience.

In a Bible college classroom, lecturers and students discuss the merits of the various kinds of preaching – topical, expository, or textual. This debate can go on and on and not reach any conclusion. However, if you have had the privilege of being part of a church for a long time and of seeing it grow in both quantity and quality so that its members become salt and light to the world, you will know what kind of preaching ministry you need to exercise in order to have a similar long-term impact. Experiencing such preaching first-hand produces far deeper convictions than classroom debates can possibly evoke.

Preaching Sermons with Freshness and Depth

I spoke earlier about pastoral preaching that transfixes its hearers. Another aspect of successful pastoral preaching is that it has ongoing freshness and depth. Many pastors are powerful the first time you hear them. In the first year of sitting under their ministry, you may even learn a lot. However, eventually the preaching begins to sound like a broken record. The sermons have a familiar ring. The same illustrations are used over and over again. You can almost finish their sermons for them because they have become so predictable. Such pastoral ministries usually do not last long. If the pastor does not move on to another pastorate, the church will become restless and push the pastor out.

What we must aim for is pastoral preaching that remains fresh for many years. Pastors who handle the Bible correctly in their preaching will have a freshness in their sermons that will make them sound more relevant to the people than the daily news. Part of the reason for this is that although the Bible was written almost two thousand years ago, it deals with issues of sin and salvation that remain relevant in every age.

The Bible is also inexhaustible. You can read the same passage over and over again, and somehow it seems that the more you read it, the more life-changing truths it reveals. A pastor who remains a student of the Bible and who reads it devotionally will have a growing depth of understanding that will spill over into the pastoral preaching.

This phenomenon is difficult to convey in a classroom situation, but if you have benefitted from good pulpit ministry you will testify that ongoing depth that inspires and stretches the hearers is a highly desirable feature of good pastoral preaching.

Later, I will go into more detail about how a pastor can maintain freshness and depth in pastoral preaching. For now, my point is simply that pastors-to-be should hear such preaching in their formative years. Without this experience they will not know that it is possible to have ongoing freshness and depth in pastoral preaching, let alone desire to have it in their own ministries.

Preaching Sermons That Meet Spiritual Needs

Pastors are like doctors. They are, in fact, physicians of souls. The church is like a hospital where patients with various ailments come to be cured. The preaching is meant to meet their spiritual needs so that they can go home better people than they were when they came in. They need to be saved from sin and helped to grow spiritually. If the preaching is not doing that, there is something seriously wrong with it.

Sadly, not all sermons meet people's spiritual needs. Many simply entertain them. These sermons are sometimes the most popular with the congregation. As the Apostle Paul warned, "the time is coming when people will not endure sound teaching, but having itching ears they will accumulate for themselves teachers to suit their own passions, and will turn away from listening to the truth and wander off into myths" (2 Tim 4:3–4). Notice that these teachers pander to what their hearers want to hear. They will let them stay in their sinful ways and will not help them spiritually.

It is a great advantage if people going into Bible college have already encountered the kind of preaching that truly meets spiritual needs. Such preaching may have helped them to overcome some sin to which they were particularly drawn. It may have caused them to think through what life is really all about and get their own priorities right. They will have seen other people turn from sin and grow into strong believers under this kind of ministry: addicts set free, marriages restored, and backsliders reclaimed. In other words, they will have seen people's personal spiritual needs met through consistent pastoral preaching.

People going into Bible college want to know how they, too, can preach such sermons and preach them effectively. They know what a tribal warrior can do with a spear and shield, and they want to be trained to become that kind of warrior for the kingdom of God. They do not simply want a job; they want to have effective ministries. To use the illustration we began with, they want to see people cured of their spiritual ailments as they preach from the life-giving Word of God. They want to be like doctors who enable patients who come to the hospital on stretchers to walk out on their own two feet instead of being carried out to the mortuary. They pray that God will enable them to be effective in a preaching ministry that will truly meet people's spiritual needs.

Combining Preaching and Practice

Pastoral preaching must be lived out in the pastor's own life. A pastor must never say, "Do as I say but never do as I do." Pastors must model the kind of simple, selfless, sacrificial Christian life they preach about. Visiting preachers may come to the church and preach one or two sermons and be gone the next day. They can make impossible demands of their hearers and make improbable claims for themselves. No one has any way of finding out whether they are speaking the truth. Pastors, however, cannot escape scrutiny. Their entire lives are in full view of the people to whom they minister.

When pastors preach about marriage, the congregation will examine the pastor's marriage. When pastors preach about bringing up children in the fear and instruction of the Lord, the church will look at the pastor's children to see if they have been moulded by the Word of God. When pastors preach about submission to all authorities, the church will want to know if the pastor truly respects the governing authorities in their village or the city. The church will also want to see that the pastor handles money and personal relationships as the Bible teaches us to, despite our fallen cravings.

The Bible must first mould our own lives before it can mould the lives of the people who will be listening to us. This is the most important thing people need to know as they enter Bible college. Their lives must be aligned with the plumb line of the Bible so that they grow up straight. Only then will they be able to convince their congregations to grow up straight too. The life of God in the soul must be visible in all aspects of the pastor's life so that the people may see how it should appear in their lives. Often this knowledge is only burned into the consciences of Bible college students if they have seen it modelled in the lives of the pastors under whose ministries they spent their formative years.

Pastors should, therefore, be conscious of the fact that while they are ministering to their congregations, their example is also moulding the lives of their congregants - including future pastors. Too many pastors fail at this. If future pastors see their pastors functioning like little chiefs in the church, they will function in the same way even if they are taught from the Bible that they should be servant leaders.

We cannot have strong churches unless the lives of pastors challenge believers to be like them as they themselves try to be like Christ. That was why the Apostle Paul wrote to the Philippians saying, "Brothers, join in imitating me, and keep your eyes on those who walk according to the example you have in us" (Phil 3:17). In doing so a congregation will be obeying what the Scriptures say: "Remember your leaders, those who spoke to you the Word of God. Consider the outcome of their way of life, and imitate their faith" (Heb 13:7).

Supporting Pastoral Internships

What we have covered in this chapter should convince us of the importance of pastoral internship programmes. Too many future pastors go into formal pastoral training without knowing what a good, three-dimensional pastoral ministry looks like. They go through Bible college training and learn a lot of theory about what is involved. Then they are thrust into pastoral leadership, and for the first time they realize that at a practical level they are woefully unprepared. They do not know what pastoral ministry really is. They preach good sermons, but they do not really know what pastoral preaching is. They are like people throwing spears into the dark hoping to hit something.

In the Bible, the Apostle Paul told Timothy, "Follow the pattern of the sound words that you have heard from me, in the faith and love that are in Christ Jesus" (2 Tim 1:13). Timothy became the man of God he was because he had spent precious time as an understudy to Paul. We see a similar pattern in the relationship between Moses and Joshua and between Elijah and Elisha. Perhaps the best example is that of Jesus and his twelve disciples whom he later commissioned as apostles. The church would certainly be stronger today if we all had the privilege of being groomed by such leaders!

Pastoral internship is especially helpful for those who have spent their formative years in less-than-ideal church situations. These make up the majority of those who go into formal training. As they go through their training, they begin to see the errors of the church context from which they came. They now know what to avoid. However, they still lack the knowledge of what to emulate because they have not seen or experienced it. But when they are exposed to pastoral ministry and pastoral preaching that approximates what they are learning in college, everything comes together beautifully. For the first time they see how they should carry out their ministry in future years so as to build a people for God.

The importance of pastoral internship, therefore, cannot be overemphasized. It is a lifesaver especially for those candidates who have not experienced good pastoral ministry themselves. Yet, there is a place for pastoral internship even for those who have been in a good church. This is because previously they saw the pastor at work only during those hours when they were not at school or at work themselves. This was usually in the evenings and over weekends. They still do not appreciate how busy pastoral ministry is during the rest of the week. They see the fruit of those hours, but not the root that produces that fruit. During pastoral internship, future pastors are given an opportunity to see close-up what makes for a successful pastoral ministry. They spend more time with a pastor and so can sense the pulse of an effective pastoral ministry. They will then better understand why pastoral preaching is so effective in transforming lives.

While I was working on this chapter, I learnt about a short video that has gone viral on the Internet. It features a Masai hunter training two young men to get an animal carcass from a pride of lions. He instructs them to be brave and to move as one, without retreating. He then goes with them as they advance towards the lions, which are about to eat their kill. The lions initially try to hold on to their prey, but are finally driven off. The hunter and his protégés cut a hunk of meat from the freshly killed animal and quickly make their escape. That is not the kind of lesson that is learnt in a classroom! You have to be with the master in the field for a while before you develop the same courage. That is what internship is supposed to achieve.

Given the rate at which the church in Africa is growing, few pastors will have the opportunity to go through full-time pastoral training. Most will have to content themselves with a few classes here and there The greatest favour we can do for such individuals is to send them for a few weeks or months to a good church where they can see, as it were, a master at work. We need to leave them there long enough for the coin to drop. The time spent in internship will prevent many casualties in the future ministry of these pastors.

Discussion Questions

1. In the light of all the advantages that a future pastor gains from seeing a successful pastor at work, what value is there in pursuing formal theological training?

2. What steps can you take if you begin to notice your preaching ministry lacking freshness and depth and a capacity to transfix its hearers?

3. How can you develop an internship programme that would enable Bible college students and others to come and understudy your ministry?

4. The family life of some pastors does not provide a good example for their congregants. What should these pastors do when they realize that their family lives are integral to their ministries?

8

Pastoral Preaching Sharpens through Training

When I was growing up, we used to have mechanical watches. That was before the digital era. The microchip had not yet been invented; everything was mechanical. I always had a very curious mind and so I wanted to know what was hidden in the compartment behind the watch face that made those hands – the hour hand, the minute hand, and the second hand – move in a circle and tell the time. One day, curiosity got the better of me and I prised open the back cover. What I found there mesmerised me. The compartment was full of metallic wheels of various sizes. Some were turning to the left, others to the right. Some were going very fast while others were moving more slowly. I had finally discovered what moved the hands of my wristwatch so that they could tell me the time! We have long lost that era in history. Today, if you open the back of your watch, you will probably find only a microchip and a battery. You won't see any moving parts.

What has all this got to do with pastoral preaching? When you are sitting in church and admiring your pastor's preaching, it is as though you are seeing the front of your wristwatch. You are seeing the effect of the many wheels in the back compartment. Your pastor's preaching is the beautiful watch face. Behind that lie years of preparation and hard work. If you are going to preach like him, you too need to have a back compartment with all those wheels in working order. Formal training at a Bible college[1] will provide those wheels – or courses – so that you will be able to accurately represent the mind of God to his people through teaching from the Bible. Let us look at some of these courses that will form part of your Bible college training.

---

1. In this chapter I use "Bible college" as a generic term for all institutions, from Bible schools to theological seminaries, where pastors receive formal training for their pastoral work.

Biblical Studies

The Biblical Studies course teaches about the Bible itself, the primary tool that you will be using in pastoral preaching. In this course you soon learn that the Bible is not one book but a library of sixty-six books. You also learn that these books are very different. Some are historical and tell us what happened at various times in the past, and especially what happened to the people of God in those times. Other books are prophetic and were written to call people back to God and warn them about what was going to happen in the future. Other books are letters that were written to churches and individuals by various church leaders. You will learn that the books of the Bible can be divided into the books of the law, history books, wisdom books, books of prophecy, gospels, epistles (or letters), and apocalyptic literature.

In Biblical Studies you come to know who wrote those books, when they were written, the circumstances that caused them to be written, who the first recipients of those books were, and the major issues that were being addressed. Some of the books are straightforward, but others are written like songs and others are written in symbols so that to understand them you need to understand the symbols and their meanings.

Why is this important for pastoral preaching? Because in the work of preaching your primary tool is the Bible. If you are going to do a good job in any trade, you must fully understand your tools. Any villager can tell you that although an axe and a hoe both consist of a wooden handle on one end and a sharp piece of metal on the other, the two are used for very different purposes. They are both very useful, but one is used for cutting trees while the other is used for ploughing the ground. It is the same with the various books of the Bible. It is very important to learn how to interpret and apply them. They each address different situations in different ways, and so must be used differently in our pastoral preaching.

For example, the book of Psalms and many of the prophetic books are written using a poetic technique called parallelism. This style of Hebrew poetry is foreign to Africans. If we do not learn to recognize it, we may misinterpret such writings and end up teaching what the original authors and the Holy Spirit who inspired them did not intend to say. We can easily end up misleading the people of God.

You will recall that one of the aims of preaching we noted earlier in this book is to help your regular listeners have a working knowledge of the Bible. This will be possible only if you yourself have a firm grasp of it.

Systematic Theology

Another important course is Systematic Theology. It covers what the Bible calls "the faith." For example, in Jude 3 we read, "Beloved, although I was very eager to write to you about our common salvation, I found it necessary to write appealing to you to contend for the faith that was once for all delivered to the saints." What did Jude mean when he said he wanted his readers to "contend for the faith"? What is "the faith" he wanted them to fight to preserve? It is the body of Christian truth. Elsewhere, the Apostle Paul refers to it as sound doctrine (Titus 1:9; 2:1). It is the full body of truth as taught in the Bible.

Systematic theology enables you to understand this body of truth. It helps you to see what the Bible teaches about God, about the Bible itself, about us as human beings, about sin and salvation, about the Christian life and the church, about the world and the way in which the world will end, and finally about heaven and hell. These topics are taught in the Bible but the teachings are scattered here and there. So there is a need to bring these scattered ideas together and set them out systematically, which is exactly what systematic theology does.

For instance, what does the Bible teach about God? There are many truths that you learn about God in the Bible. One of them is that he is Father, Son, and Holy Spirit – three persons but one God. The Father is God, the Son is God, and the Holy Spirit is God. Yet there are not three Gods but one. How do we know that? Is it because there is one verse somewhere in the Bible that teaches all that? No. We learn this by putting together all the verses in the Bible that teach about the Father, the Son, and the Holy Spirit. When we harmonize all these verses, we cannot help but come away with the understanding that God is three-in-one. That is what systematic theology does for you. However, it goes beyond teaching us about God. It covers all the major teachings of the Bible.

Why is it important for a person who engages in pastoral preaching to be trained in systematic theology? Because preachers who have not been taught to see the whole body of truth that is taught in the Bible may misinterpret a verse or passage. For instance, they may read a verse about the death of Jesus and conclude that he cannot be God because God does not die. Or they may go to a verse that teaches that God is one and conclude that therefore Jesus and the Holy Spirit are not God. Systematic theology helps you to teach Christian doctrine accurately. That is very important if you are going to help believers to grow spiritually.

Systematic theology is also helpful because it is closely related to two of the goals of pastoral preaching. You want your regular listeners to develop a comprehensive view of the gospel and to have an appreciation of sound doctrine. This will happen only when you as a pastoral preacher are truly grounded in Christian doctrine.

Church History

The Acts of the Apostles records the founding of the church and its early years. But what happened after that? In Church History you learn the answer to this question as you survey the development and spread of the church over the past two thousand years. You learn about the primary leaders and teachers whom the apostles left behind to continue pastoring the church when it was still in its infancy. You learn about some of the early doctrinal conflicts that arose in the church and how they were addressed. You learn about how the church spread throughout the world from the first century to the present day. You see that there were times when the spiritual life in the church was almost dead, and how God revived it through evangelistic and pastoral preaching. You learn all these things and more.

Why is it important for you to learn all these things? I ask this question because many of us are not interested in history. Why should I learn about things that happened hundreds of years ago in Europe when I live in Africa in the twenty-first century? What relevance does it have to my ministry in Africa today? To use our wristwatch analogy, how does this wheel in the back compartment contribute to the accurate telling of the time?

There are many advantages to learning about church history. One of them is that it helps us to avoid repeating the mistakes of the past. Almost all the current doctrinal errors being propagated in the church through defective pastoral preaching are repetitions of errors that have cropped up in the church in the past and were settled with the help of the Holy Spirit and Holy Scripture. They change their form a little and put on more modern clothing but they are essentially the same. Once you learn about those mistakes and how they affected the life of the church, you will want to keep away from them in your pastoral preaching.

More positively, in studying church history you also learn about the individuals whom God used to bring spiritual health to his church in times past. You see how they laboured faithfully in pastoral preaching. This inspires you in your own ministry. You want to emulate them. In Hebrews 13:7 we read, "Remember your leaders, those who spoke to you the Word of God. Consider the outcome of their way of life, and imitate their faith." In church history we see the outcome of the ministries of those who spoke the Word of God faithfully and are challenged to do the same today.

Other Courses

There are other courses that are taught in Bible college, but my aim in this chapter is not to give you the full menu but rather to show you how having formal training goes a long way to making you a better preacher to the people of God. Let me briefly refer to two other courses – Pastoral Studies and Biblical Languages.

In Pastoral Studies (sometimes called Practical Theology) you are taught about the work of a pastor. This includes, among other lessons, how God calls you to the work of a pastor, how to maintain your spiritual walk, how to prepare and preach sermons, how to visit church members and counsel them, and how to lead the church in general. You do not need to be a genius to see how relevant such studies are to pastoral preaching. After all, it is in this course that you even learn how to preach good sermons!

In Biblical Languages, you learn about the languages in which the Bible was originally written. I hope you know that the Bible was not written in English. The Old Testament was originally written in Hebrew and the New Testament in Greek. Here and there some other languages were used, but these two were the primary languages used in writing the Bible. Of course the Bible has now been translated into the various languages of the world. The translators go back to the original Hebrew and Greek texts and then translate those original words into a language that you are able to read and understand.

The advantage of learning some basic Hebrew and Greek is that you are able to do some of that work yourself. For example, in Greek culture there were many words for the word "love." Some of them are *eros* (which the Bible never uses, but the concept is there), *phileo*, and *agape*. *Eros* is sexual love, *phileo* is brotherly love, and *agape* is unconditional love. You will teach and apply God's Word more accurately if you know which kind of love is being referred to when, for instance, the Bible says, "Love one another." Is it sexual love, brotherly love, or unconditional love?

Thankfully, today there are many aids to help us to understand and interpret the biblical text. There are Bible commentaries, interlinear Bibles, Bible dictionaries, and so on. These are written and compiled by experts who have spent many years studying the Bible and we benefit from their learning. However, if you are able to learn some Hebrew and Greek, it will help you to do your own homework and to understand what is being said in the text of Scripture yourself.

Because of financial and educational constraints, many of you reading this book may never have the opportunity to learn any of these original biblical languages. However, it is good for you to know why learning them is such a great help to pastoral preaching.

Further Benefits of Training

Spending time in Bible college forces you to read books that you would not normally read in the course of your pastoral ministry. This stretches your knowledge base and can only enrich your ministry in years to come. In college you are forced to work hard to keep pace with programme deadlines. This develops your reading and thinking capacity. It is the difference between running on your own (or going jogging) and being coached for a race. When you are being prepared for a race, the coach will push you and you will have to stretch yourself and see how fast your muscles and sinews can enable you to run. This enables you to do your best. That is what studying in a structured course does for you. You will accomplish far more than you could on your own.

We began with an analogy of a wristwatch and the world of wheels hidden in the watchcase. Let us get back there as we come to the end of this chapter. What we are interested in seeing when we look at the watch are the hands, because it is the hands that tell the time. Only watchmakers and the watch repairers need to know about the world of wheels in the back compartment. In the same way, the church members who listen to your preaching will not be interested in your systematic theology or church history. They want to know from you what the Bible is saying and how they can apply it to their daily lives so that they can live in a way that glorifies God. So, do not bore them with all the technical stuff that you learnt in college. That is for you – the expert. When you teach them doctrine, base your teaching on the particular text of Scripture that you are preaching from. If you refer to church history, do so because it illustrates the truth that you are seeing in the biblical text. Only tell your listeners what the Hebrew or Greek says in the original Scriptures if there is something very important that is not obvious in the version you are preaching from. Sometimes, as pastors wanting to show off how much we know, we clutter our sermons with so much information that our listeners fail to see the simple truths that God wants to communicate to them. In other words, we expose the wheels in the back compartment so much that the hands of the watch are not easy to see anymore. It is very impressive, but people are unable to easily tell the time.

Having said that, never underestimate the importance of the wheels in the back compartment for you as the expert. If the watch is going to be accurate in telling the time for a very long time, it has to have very good wheels. When I was growing up, the reliability of a watch was often determined by the number of jewels it had. The jewels reduced the friction between moving parts and so extended the accuracy of the watch for many more years. The more jewels a watch had the more valuable it was. That is how it is with us as preachers too. The more firmly grounded we are in all these areas of learning that contribute to accurate pastoral preaching, the more we will be true and reliable teachers of the Word of God. So, if you can find the time and money, go through formal Bible college training. It will be for your good and for the good of those who will be listening to your pastoral preaching.

Discussion Questions

1. In some parts of the Majority World, there are very few Western-type Bible colleges. What should an individual do who wants to have formal pastoral training but cannot access such colleges?

2. What advice can you give to a pastor or a potential pastor who is not literate but wants to be trained to be an effective pastoral preacher?

3. There are many Bible colleges. What criteria should a person use to find a reputable college?

4. What other courses are often taught in Bible colleges and how can they help you in pastoral preaching?

9

Pastoral Preaching Matures through Fellowship

Some preachers get better with time while others only get worse. The former are like wine, which I am told gets better with age. The others are like ordinary food, which rots if it is not refrigerated. If you are a pastor and desire to build a people for God over the long haul, I know that you hope to belong to the first category – getting better with time. Yet hoping is not enough, there are a number of "helps" that you will need in order for you to go from strength to strength. Not all of them will be available to you all the time. However, you would do well to make use of as many of them as the Lord brings your way.

In trying to find a common term for these "helps," I have found the word "fellowship" the most appropriate. Pastoral preachers grow and mature by interacting with other pastoral preachers. After initially learning the art from their own pastors in their formative years and honing their skills through Bible college training, they need to grow into maturity as a preacher. This maturing will happen only as they continue to interact with those who have either become good preachers themselves, or have had their spiritual taste buds trained over time to tell the difference between good and bad preaching. Ongoing fellowship with such individuals will have a lasting positive effect on a pastor's preaching.

In the book of Proverbs, the Bible says, "Iron sharpens iron, and one man sharpens another" (Prov 27:17). It also says, "Whoever walks with the wise becomes wise, but the companion of fools will suffer harm" (Prov 13:20). These sayings teach that the kind of company we keep will make us either better or worse in years to come. This is true for pastors too. We need the kind of fellowship around us that will enhance our preaching ministry. This fellowship can come in a number of different ways.

Reading Books on Preaching

One of the ways in which you will continue to grow in your pastoral preaching is by reading books on preaching. God has given his servants various gifts. Some who have the gift of teaching have been training pastors for many years in the art of preaching, or homiletics as it is called in academic circles. Sometimes these people publish their lecture materials as books. There are also experienced pastors who, after many years in pastoral ministry, take time to analyse what has enabled them to be successful as pastoral preachers and write this down for the benefit of others.

Today, some very experienced pastors are also maintaining Internet blogs in which they share some of their pastoral experiences. If you have access to the Internet, you should consider asking other pastors what blogs they are finding helpful, especially in the area of shepherding God's flock, and then visit and read those blogs yourself. But remember that not all blogs are helpful. So, ask pastors whose ministries you really respect to suggest a few helpful blogs to you. That is a good place to start.

I can think of three examples of very successful pastors from the twentieth century who have left their thoughts on preaching in writing. The Welsh preacher Dr Martyn Lloyd-Jones was asked to give a series of lectures on preaching in the USA after he had been engaged in preaching at Westminster Chapel in London for some forty years. His lectures were published in a book entitled *Preaching and Preachers.*[1] John Stott also wrote a classic on preaching after many years of pastoring All Souls Church in Langham Place, London. The book has undergone a few title changes, but the most well-known title is *I Believe in Preaching.*[2] John Piper wrote the book, *The Supremacy of God in Preaching*, which was a distillation of his passion for preaching, after thirty-three years of pastoring Bethlehem Baptist Church in Minneapolis, Minnesota.[3] If you can get hold of these titles written by very successful

---

1. Grand Rapids: Zondervan, 1972.

2. Shortly before his death, John Stott approved an abridged and updated version of this book. John Stott and Greg Scharf, *I Believe in Preaching* (Carlisle; Langham Preaching Resources, 2013 / Grand Rapids: Eerdmans, 2015)

3. Grand Rapids: Baker, 2015.

pastoral preachers, do so. However, there are also many other great books on preaching that will help you to improve your preaching.

The best time to read about preaching is when you are on holiday or on leave. That is a good time to take a few books and work your way through them. Like a subsistence farmer who harvests a crop and stores it so that he can draw from it until the next harvest, you are reading to practically apply the lessons you will be learning in the next phase of your ministry until your next holiday or leave. While on leave, you will not be under pressure because you are resting from your usual work. So you will have time to think deeply about how to apply what you are learning from the books.

But what can you do if, like many pastors in Africa, you do not have the money to keep buying books on preaching and cannot download books from the Internet? Borrowing is one option. You can ask a fellow pastor to lend you a book on preaching, which you should promise to return when your leave or holiday is over. (And you should keep that promise, and not end up being the proverbial African "book-keeper"!)

Learning from Others in Pastors' Fraternals

Another source of ongoing maturation for you as a pastoral preacher is fellow pastors who are currently serving in your locality. "No man is an island." We often speak about the need for fellowship among ordinary Christians by referring to red-hot coals that burn longer when they are heaped together on a brazier. When one piece is removed from the others and left on its own, it soon becomes cold. Well, what is good for your church members is also good for you as a pastor. If you are going to keep growing in your preaching work, you need to spend time with other pastors.

Pastors' fraternals are places where different "how to" topics are discussed – how to work with other church elders, how to counsel church members in different situations, and so on. Practical topics related to preaching are also discussed, such as how to handle sensitive subjects in sermons, preaching from difficult passages, using illustrations to liven up your preaching, and so on. Usually, the pastors in your fraternal will each share from their area of expertise, so you will have a large pool of fellow pastors to learn from.[4]

---

4. Langham Preaching, which fosters biblical preaching movements all over the world, also encourages the formation of local "preachers clubs," in which preachers get together regularly to sharpen their skills in biblical preaching. It there is such a club in your area, join

The advantage of pastors' fraternals over reading books is that you can go to your next fraternal meeting with the questions that are currently dogging you, and your fellow pastors there can help you with very practical answers. Usually one pastor will present on a topic, and there will be questions and discussion afterwards. The person teaching is a live teacher in the same room with you, and because these are fellow pastors whom you meet regularly, you are free to ask questions without fear of looking foolish. So, although the individuals in your fraternal may not be as gifted and experienced as the authors who have written books, you will profit from this kind of collective interaction.

Therefore, as soon as you are settled in a locality, find out from the pastors in your area if there is a pastors' fraternal there. See how you can tailor your weekly or monthly schedule so that you are able to attend as many of their meetings as possible. You may not agree with the doctrinal positions of everyone in the group, but you can be sure that because you are pastors serving a common community, there will be a lot you can learn from the others. Remember the illustration of the burning coal.

Listening to Good Preaching

We said earlier that good preaching is more caught than taught. This is not only true when a person is sitting under the ministry of a pastor in their formative years; it is also true in later years when one is already in pastoral ministry. As you listen to other people preaching, something of their preaching rubs off on you. So, you do well to make it a deliberate policy to listen to good preaching as often as you possibly can.

Granted, there are often not many good preachers around for you to listen to every time you have a free Sunday. However, if you do have one or two, make it a priority to attend their churches and listen to them. If the good preachers are in another town, plan to visit their churches when you are on leave.

You can also listen to recordings of good preaching on CDs, DVDs or the Internet. (Once I would have talked about sermons being stored on audiotapes, but that technology is seldom used these days. I do not know how much longer we will have CDs and DVDs either.) You can listen to these sermons in your own home and profit immensely from them.

---

it. If not, find out how you can start one. You will find it very helpful in sharpening your preaching skills.

Whereas ordinary Christians will be seeking only to learn the lessons in the sermons they hear, you will be seeking to learn the communication strategies as well. You will be listening to the technical side of the sermons so that you can learn a few lessons to improve your own preaching. Listen to how other preachers introduce their sermons to see how you can be more effective in capturing the attention of your hearers at the start of your sermons. Take note of the way they transition from one point to another, and how they logically argue their points. Pay careful attention to their ability to turn the ears of their listeners into eyes by using illustrations and the like. Observe the way they apply their sermons and bring them to a powerful close. See what you can glean from all this to improve your own sermon delivery. Even when you listen to a very poor sermon, you can learn what not to do in your own preaching. So you can learn even from bad sermons!

Attending Conferences and Seminars

Yet another way in which you can mature into a very effective pastoral preacher is by attending conferences and seminars on preaching. I once sat on the Medical Council of Zambia, where I learnt that medical professionals have to renew their licences every few years. In order for their applications for renewal to be approved, they have to show proof that they have attended at least one seminar or workshop relevant to their field of work within a specified period. This was in order to make sure that they were keeping up with developments in their field as they continued to attend to patients. If ongoing training is seen as important for those who attend to our physical bodies that will die, surely it must be even more important for those of us who attend to never-dying souls that can end up in hell forever due to our failure.

At conferences and seminars the speakers are usually experts on the subjects on which they are presenting. Those speaking on preaching will have been chosen because they teach homiletics, or have many years of experience in preaching, or both. Often, these individuals have written on the subject of preaching, and they will share material from their books and blogs at the conference or seminar. It will be like listening to an audiobook with the author right in front of you. You will have the opportunity to ask questions and get very helpful answers.

When such gifted and experienced servants of God are brought close to you, you should see this as God's giving you an opportunity to grow in your preaching ministry. It is important to budget for such events because most of them are not free. It takes a lot of money to bring such servants of God to your region, and some of that money will have to be recouped from those who are going to profit from their ministry. Make space in your busy schedule to attend these teaching sessions. Do not look at your academic qualifications and feel too proud to be seen in a group that is learning how to preach or how to preach better. The one or two extra hints you will learn from such conferences and seminars will help you to become a better pastoral preacher.

Listening to Constructive Criticism

One source of growth for pastoral preaching that is rarely thought about is constructive criticism. It is not pleasant to hear people tell you that if your preaching does not improve, you will empty your church. That is why most people prefer to gossip about our poor preaching rather than tell us about it. They understand this human dynamic. After all, they are also human. However, when people love us and mean well, their negative comments about our preaching can be a real blessing. These constructive critics are criticizing us in order to make us better.

There are some aspects of preaching that you cannot learn from books or from other pastors or from listening to other people's sermons or even by attending seminars. These are aspect of your preaching that even you may not be aware of. For instance, perhaps you often rub your nose when you are preaching, or keep saying "you know" in the middle of your sentences, or keep mispronouncing a word, or shout too much, or need to raise your voice so that people at the back can hear you, or maybe a tinge of vindictiveness has crept into your preaching. The list is endless. You need other people to point these out to you because often you are blissfully ignorant of them.

If you are a married man, your wife will probably be your best critic. She looks you over before you leave the house to make sure that you look presentable as you stand before God's people. She listens to your sermons very carefully and gets concerned if you keep making the same mistakes or send people to sleep. While others may not be bold enough to bring this matter to your attention, your wife will do so. A man is wise who listens to his wife. She can only mean well. After all, she wants her husband to succeed as a pastor, and she knows that preaching is an important part of how a congregation judge the pastor's competence.

If you have other church leaders or elders who work with you in the church, ask for their input as well. You do not need to ask all of them; choose those who are full of wisdom and experience. You also do not need to ask them to give you feedback every time you preach. Rather, let them know that you appreciate their feedback whenever they have something to say about your preaching, or simply ask them every so often for their judicious opinion on your preaching. Where you do not have such individuals in your own church, try to find mentors outside your church to fulfil this role. You could send them your sermons whenever you need their input. This is especially important in the first five to ten years of your preaching ministry, before you cut your teeth in the work, because once bad habits are formed they are very difficult to change.

It is wise to practice this openness with your church leaders, especially in the African context where church members will not have the courage to talk to you about your preaching. In our cultures, people are genuinely afraid to say anything negative about their leaders, especially to their face, and so pastors will rarely hear criticism from their congregation. This has been worsened by the "man of God" phenomenon that has become commonplace, where pastors are believed to have strange mystical powers and so are feared in precisely the same way that village people fear witch doctors. However, members will complain to the other leaders, and if your leaders know that you are not too sensitive to such feedback, they will bring it to your attention and you will be able to work on strengthening those areas of weakness. Your pastoral preaching can only get better because of this.

Discussion Questions

1. What can we do to motivate and encourage a reading culture among pastors?

2. How can you go about starting or maintaining a pastors' fraternal that can truly enrich the ministries of pastors in your area?

3. The Apostle Paul told Timothy to fan into flame the gift of God in him (2 Tim 1:6). Apart from the areas covered in this chapter, in what other ways can you fan into flame the gift of preaching that is in you?

4. What can we do to enable ordinary members of our congregation to feel free to give us constructive criticism?

Section D

The Challenges of Pastoral Preaching

10

Preaching and Praying as Spiritual Warfare

Knowing your enemy is key to knowing how to defeat your enemy. Let me give you an example of this. Pioneer missionary work in Africa used to be very dangerous. African chiefs were suspicious of anything new and of anyone from outside their immediate tribe, which made their reactions unpredictable. Then there were the dangers posed by wild animals and snakes. To cap all this, malaria killed more missionaries than the African chiefs and wildlife combined. For many years, no one knew what caused malaria and so it was almost impossible to combat it. All that could be done was to try to treat the symptoms with quinine. It was not until 1880 that the parasite causing malaria was finally identified. That was a major breakthrough. Then in 1897 came the discovery that the parasite was spread by the *Anopheles* mosquito. Since then, much effort has been put into finding ways to eradicate this mosquito and protect people from being bitten. Recently, there has been a big push to encourage people to sleep under mosquito nets that have been treated with an insecticide. As a result of these measures, thousands of lives have been saved. Knowing the enemy has made it possible to attack and defeat the enemy.

We as pastoral preachers also have an enemy we need to be working hard to defeat. What is this enemy? It is our fallen human nature.

Fallen Human Nature

Some of you may be wondering why I identified fallen human nature as our enemy, rather than the devil (who is sometimes called Satan in the Bible). There is no doubt that he is a very real enemy. The Bible refers to him as a deceiver because he often uses deception to lure us away from God's perfect law. That was the technique he used to bring about the fall of our first parents, Adam and Eve. He has an even easier job with us, because we already have a fallen nature. That is what he appeals to when he tempts us, and that is why we give in so easily.

This same fallen human nature results in our being tempted by things in the world around us. We listen to gossip or to whispers about opportunities for dishonest gain, we look at pictures of objects or bodies that we covet, and so allow ourselves to be drawn away from God's righteous laws. It is as if we have swallowed a magnet and find ourselves being attracted to all the metal objects around us. Our fallen nature draws us towards a fallen world.

According to the Bible, we are all born with a fallen nature that leads us to rebel against God and his law. We are naturally ungodly and unrighteous. But when we become Christians, we are cleansed by the blood of Christ and the almighty power of his Spirit. Our sinful nature is defeated! But in Africa we know all too well that even a defeated enemy can still conduct raids and spread havoc. And that is what happens in our lives. Our sinful nature is defeated, but it is not yet eradicated. It is still at work within us. Even as great a man as the Apostle Paul had to admit, "I do not understand my own actions. For I do not do what I want, but I do the very thing I hate. Now if I do what I do not want, I agree with the law, that it is good. So now it is no longer I who do it, but sin that dwells within me" (Rom 7:15–17).

The enemy we must contend with in pastoral preaching is thus the "sin that dwells within," that is, within us and within the hearts of those to whom we preach. It stands in the way of building a people for God because it causes believers to serve the world and the devil instead of living for the glory of God. The task of pastoral preaching is to reverse that tendency so that God's people can live for God's glory despite this enemy within, until God himself removes its presence when he glorifies his people in eternity.

Supernatural Power

The bad news is that sin affects all of us. Here is the good news: God has the supernatural power to deal with sin, and the tools he uses to accomplish this are prayer and pastoral preaching. If it were not for this reality, we should have despaired long ago. How can you get into the human heart and do a spiritual operation to remove sin? It is impossible! But God is almighty. He can do all things. He has given us the weapons to do his supernatural work.

Perhaps the most encouraging evidence of this is found in the relationship of the Apostle Paul to the church in Corinth. It was a church that he established (see Acts 18). Later, other preachers such as Apollos and the Apostle Peter laboured there. However, it took a long time for this church to function well. When Paul wrote his first letter to Corinth, the church was full of divisions around the personalities of its missionary pastors, and there were serious cases of sexual immorality, drunkenness and gluttony, fights over spiritual gifts, and so on. Could anything be worse than this?

How did the Apostle Paul address this? Did he go in and simply close down the church? No. He tells us what his tactics were: "The weapons of our warfare are not of the flesh but have divine power to destroy strongholds. We destroy arguments and every lofty opinion raised against the knowledge of God, and take every thought captive to obey Christ, being ready to punish every disobedience, when your obedience is complete" (2 Cor 10:4–6).

Paul was a human leader but he was not going to react to problems in the same way that other human leaders do. In politics, leaders sometimes command armies and use physical weapons to put down rebellion. Or they may try to use slander to ruin the careers of those who oppose them. But Paul does not resort to such tactics. Rather, God had given him (and the other Christian leaders) spiritual weapons capable of putting down any rebellion in human hearts. Using these weapons, they could bring down anything that was against the true knowledge of God and bring people to their knees before the cross of Christ. Once those who were truly God's children had been moved to obey God, Paul and others would exercise church discipline by way of excommunicating those who remained stubborn in their disobedience.

Let us now look more closely at how God uses preaching and praying to unleash his supernatural power on human hearts.

Preaching

In the book of Ephesians, the Apostle Paul writes about the armour of God. Almost all of that armour – the belt, the breastplate, the shoes, the shield, and the helmet – is intended to defend the one wearing it. However, there is one part of the armour that is used in attack. It is "the sword of the Spirit, which is the Word of God" (Eph 6:17).

Granted, in this passage Paul was not writing about preaching but about how every believer should be able to stand when under attack by the evil one. But the battle that is going on is the same battle against sin that preachers' have to fight. The devil wants us to sin against God. The Word of God is the weapon that we should be using to vanquish him. It has supernatural power because it is the Word of God. So the Apostle Paul was urging the Ephesians to call the Word of God to mind when they were under intense temptation and trial. It has power to defeat the world, the flesh, and the devil. Similarly, we as pastors should wield the sword of the Word of God to arrest sin in their hearts in the lives of believers.

When God called Jeremiah to be his prophet he said to him, "Behold, I have put my words in your mouth. See, I have set you this day over nations and over kingdoms, to pluck up and to break down, to destroy and to overthrow, to build and to plant" (Jer 1:9–10). What weapon did God give Jeremiah to enable him to do all these things? Only the words that God put in his mouth. Jeremiah had no other weapon. This too is an indication of how powerful the Word of God is in the hearts of human beings.

Paul too had great confidence when he preached the Word of God. He refused to use tricks to attract people, for "we have renounced disgraceful, underhanded ways. We refuse to practice cunning or to tamper with God's Word, but by the open statement of the truth we would commend ourselves to everyone's conscience in the sight of God" (2 Cor 4:2). Paul simply preached Christ and him crucified and left the results to God:

> And I, when I came to you, brothers, did not come proclaiming to you the testimony of God with lofty speech or wisdom. For I decided to know nothing among you except Jesus Christ and him crucified. And I was with you in weakness and in fear and much trembling, and my speech and my message were not in plausible words of wisdom, but in demonstration of the Spirit and of power, so that your faith might not rest in the wisdom of men but in the power of God. (1 Cor 2:1–5)

So, settle it in your mind that the Word of God has divine power. Preach it! Sadly, many pastors are losing sight of this fact. There is a growing misconception that the power of God is demonstrated only when people are called to the front for prayer. However, the preached Word of God powerfully changes lives in a way that no other communication is able to. This happens when the Spirit of God takes the Word that you are proclaiming and applies it to human hearts. That is what Paul meant when he spoke about preaching "in demonstration of the Spirit and of power."

Remember that in Ephesians 6 the Apostle Paul referred to the Word of God as the sword of the Spirit. As you preach, the Spirit of God effectively uses the Word of God to kill sin in human hearts and to instil the fear of God.

Praying

Let us take another look at the armour of God as explained by the Apostle Paul in Ephesians 6. Notice that prayer is very closely associated with the Word of God:

> Take the helmet of salvation, and the sword of the Spirit, which is the Word of God, praying at all times in the Spirit, with all prayer and supplication. To that end keep alert with all perseverance, making supplication for all the saints, and also for me, that words may be given to me in opening my mouth boldly to proclaim the mystery of the gospel, for which I am an ambassador in chains, that I may declare it boldly, as I ought to speak. (Eph 6:17–20)

You cannot miss the fact that prayer plays a vital role in this offensive against sin in human hearts. The Apostle Paul asked the Ephesians to pray "at all times in the Spirit, with all prayer and supplication" for all the saints. He did not mean that they should pray in tongues at all times, but rather that they should pray with the help of the Spirit of God. This is what he meant in Romans 8 when he wrote, "Likewise the Spirit helps us in our weakness. For we do not know what to pray for as we ought, but the Spirit himself intercedes for us with groanings too deep for words. And he who searches hearts knows what is the mind of the Spirit, because the Spirit intercedes for the saints according to the will of God" (Rom 8:26–27). This is praying in total dependence on the Spirit of God. It is the equivalent of preaching in total dependence on the Spirit of God.

Notice also that the Apostle Paul asked for prayer for his own preaching. He asked the believers in Ephesus to pray that God would give him the right words and courage as he preached. We preach to human minds. We communicate with them in words. God alone is able to give us the right words so that we can be understood. God is able to also give us the right arguments to answer questions that are arising in human minds even as they listen to us. This is all part of the way in which God brings people to abandon sin and live for him. He does not bypass the mind. He prevails upon the heart through the mind. We are persuaded about the error of sin as we hear it explained, and consequently we abandon it and accept God's salvation. That is how we are saved and that is also how we are sanctified. So Paul was asking the Ephesian believers to pray for him to have the right words and to be courageous enough to speak them.

Preaching and prayer go together. That was why the apostles spent a lot of time in these two activities. When the church grew to the point where other duties such as caring for widows became urgent, they chose to hand over those tasks to others rather than compromise their preaching and prayer. They told the church, "It is not right that we should give up preaching the Word of God to serve tables. Therefore, brothers, pick out from among you seven men of good repute, full of the Spirit and of wisdom, whom we will appoint to this duty. But we will devote ourselves to prayer and to the ministry of the word" (Acts 6:2–4). Prayer and the ministry of the word re like a left and right foot. They go together.

While we will ask the church and other believers to pray for us as we preach, we must also pray for ourselves. As we prepare, we should pray that God will give us his message for his people. We should also pray for our sermon delivery, that as we stand up to speak God will give us the right words to communicate his truths and his will to our hearers. We should pray that the Spirit of God will use the words we speak to save the lost and to sanctify his people. Yes, we should pray that he will pull down the strongholds of sin in human hearts and instead erect temples there in which only the worship of God will be entertained. We should pray that through our preaching God will build a people for himself – a people who are holy and living for his own glory.

Our God is a prayer-answering God. Where there is genuine dependence on him and trust in him, he acknowledges the prayers of his people and does a supernatural work. Fallen human nature will be defeated in human hearts and God will be exalted in its place. We will return to the subject of prayer in chapter 17, for it is an important source of power for the preaching ministry.

Go about your ministry of pastoral preaching knowing that ultimately it is not dependent on your cleverness or your oratorical powers but on the Word of God and the Spirit of God. Your role is to preach and pray, and then leave everything to God. He will do the supernatural work.

At the start of this chapter, I said that knowing our enemy goes a long way in helping us to defeat the enemy. The sin in human hearts is your enemy. In your own strength you cannot defeat it. You need divine power. Thankfully, this is available to you through preaching and praying. Be sure to use it!

Discussion Questions

1. How does a lack of awareness of the depravity of the human heart affect how you go about your sermon preparation and delivery?

2. What do you understand by supernatural power, especially as it relates to the work of preaching?

3. What effect has listening to preaching that was empowered by God had on your life?

4. What activities do pastors in your area often resort to in an attempt to add power or effectiveness to their preaching?

11

Studying How to Preach Well

In chapter 9, we looked at how pastoral preaching matures through fellowship with other preachers. I recommended that you read books on preaching and learn from others who are in pastoral ministry. I emphasized the need to listen to good preaching and to attend conferences and seminars on preaching. Finally, I talked about the need to listen to constructive criticism, especially from those who have been preaching for some time. All these suggestions help us to become better preachers.

We always need to remember that preaching is a form of communication, and as such, it is both a science and an art. Not everyone is born with the talents that can make them a great preacher, just as not everyone is born with the talent to be a world-class musician. But most of us could learn to play a musical instrument if we had a good teacher, and in the same way most of us can learn techniques that will make us become better preachers, preachers whom people will want to listen to. This was true of Ezekiel, who was said to be like "one who sings lover songs with a beautiful voice and plays an instrument well" (Ezek 33:32 NIV). People wanted to hear what he had to say, even if they did not bother to apply it to their lives.

If you master the techniques that make for communication, you will be able to communicate well. If you ignore them, you will fail to communicate the Word of God to your hearers even if you think you are "full of the Holy Spirit." Hence, as you learn from other preachers, be alert to how they use these techniques to make their preaching compelling. You will then see how you can employ those same techniques to improve your own preaching.

Mastering the Use of Words

The most basic ingredient of verbal communication is words. In preaching we use words. Words are to preaching what balls are to football. When I was a boy, I loved playing football with my friends. It was our favourite pastime. Often, one person owned the ball and so when we wanted to play football we would go to his home and ask for his ball. He rarely gave us the ball without coming along to play too. Since the ball was his, we were very careful how we tackled him. Every so often he would be tackled badly, or his side would be losing, or he would simply be in a bad mood. Then he would suddenly pick up the ball and begin walking home. We would plead with him and sometimes manage to persuade him to stay. But often we failed and that was the end of the game! We could not go on playing without the ball. We all learnt to be in the good books of the guy who owned the ball. Sometimes the owner of the ball would arrive on the football grounds and see someone he disliked. He would insist that this person should not play with his ball. The rest of us had no choice but to ask the boy to leave. The owner of the ball often abused his ownership in this way. We despised him for it, but we needed his ball and so we still begged him to be with us. Without a ball, football was impossible.

Preaching is like that. In order to be an effective preacher you must be a good friend of words. You must master the use of them. One way to do this is simply by reading a lot. Read newspaper and magazine articles and books written by popular authors. The reason these authors are popular is that they know how to communicate their ideas in appealing ways. Listen also to popular preachers, even if you do not agree with their doctrines. Notice how they are able to express their thoughts with just the right words, and resolve to do the same in your own preaching. Some preachers use big words that no one understands. That may prop up their egos because it gives people the impression that they are very educated, but it does not add anything to their ability to communicate. That is not good for preaching because in preaching your chief goal is not to display your education but to communicate God's Word to his people. It is vital that you learn to use the words that best turn on the lights in the brains of your hearers. You want them to understand the Word of God so that they can obey God.

A good companion as you study how to use words is what is called a thesaurus. This is like a dictionary. But whereas a dictionary gives you the meaning of a word, a thesaurus gives you alternatives to that word to help you express your ideas as precisely as possible. Here's how it works. You have an idea that you want to communicate but cannot quite put it into words. A word you have in mind doesn't seem quite right. Look up the word that you are currently thinking of in a thesaurus and you will see other words that are similar in meaning. Then choose from the list the word that best expresses what you want to say.

Crafting an Introduction, Body and Conclusion

If you are to preach well, you must also master the way in which you use words in the introduction, the body, and the conclusion of your sermons. The introduction is like a plane taxiing out onto the runway before a flight. The main body is like the plane in the air. It has taken off and is in full flight. The conclusion is like the plane landing and taxiing to the gate where the passengers will disembark. All these stages of a flight are important if the plane is to deliver its passengers safely to their desired destination. Good sermons, too, must do a good job in each of those three stages – the introduction, the main body, and the conclusion.

The introduction of your sermon must not only introduce your text or topic but must also grip the attention of your hearers so that they want to listen to the rest of the sermon. Finding good introductions is easier for roving evangelists because they can repeat the same few good ones as they move from one audience to another. Pastoral preachers do not have that luxury because they preach to the same audience every week. So it takes a little more effort to prepare good introductions and to have enough variety to keep your audience's attention week after week. When you listen to good preachers, listen carefully to the ways in which they introduce their sermons. See how you can improve your preaching by employing what you learn from them.

Then there is the body of your sermon. Here you want to ensure that your main message is fully understood and is presented persuasively so that your hearers will apply it. This means that your sermon cannot just be a jumble of ideas, no matter how important those ideas are. There must be a clear structure to the main body of your sermon, with sub-points that follow logically from one to the next so that your hearers sense that they are moving forward and not going around in circles. For example, if you are expounding a passage of Scripture, your sub-points may parallel the text of the passage that is being explained, although that is not the only possible structure.

Finally, there is the conclusion of your sermon. The plane must land. It must deliver what it promised. For many preachers this is the most difficult part of the sermon. Their conclusions tend to be either too abrupt or they say "lastly" and then they last forever! Like an airplane, they seem to either crash-land or simply continue circling in the air until they run out of fuel. So pay careful attention to your conclusion. It should concisely summarize the main points of your sermon and should include its final major application. That way your hearers will go away knowing clearly what God was saying to them and what God wants them to do in response.

Using Illustrations and Applications

Some sermons are interesting and keep you captivated from beginning to end, while others are "heavy" and dull, making you long for the end. What explains the difference? Apart from an attention-grabbing introduction, a logical main body, and a gripping conclusion, there are two other elements that make a sermon interesting. These are illustrations and applications.

Illustrations are to sermons what windows are to buildings. They engage the imagination of your listeners. If you were in a room with the curtains closed and I was to describe to you the beautiful garden outside, it would take a lot of mental energy for you to appreciate the beauty of that garden. If I simply opened the curtains, you would say, "Wow!" because your eyes would see the garden in all its beauty. That is what illustrations do. They make the eyes of your mind "see" the point that is being made in the sermon. For instance, you can teach about the authority of the Lord Jesus Christ by explaining what he says we should do or not do in the Bible, and your congregation will be trying to understand the concept. However, if you illustrate that concept with an example of authority in everyday life, you will see their faces light up. For example, you could illustrate Christ's authority by comparing it to that of a traffic cop. When a traffic cop raises his or her hand to stop your car, you stop. If they indicate that you should pull off the road and park, you do so. They carry with them the authority of your president.

Some preachers are better at using illustrations than others. Jesus was a master at this. His parables were actually illustrations. By the time he finished his stories, his listeners understood more about the kingdom of heaven than they would have done if he had continued teaching in abstract terms. He was the perfect teacher and we do well to learn from him. We can also learn from other preachers who use illustrations well. There are even books and Web sites on the art of sermon illustrations. We must continue to study how we can use illustrations to keep our sermons interesting to our hearers.

Apart from illustrations, there are also applications. These make the sermon relevant to the hearers. Remember that the Bible was written thousands of years ago. If all you are doing is explaining what it teaches, your hearers may feel as if you are a teacher giving them a history lesson. They may not sense that God is speaking to them in the here and now. They may lose interest in your sermon. But when you apply the Word of Got to them as you preach, they will realize that it is about them. They will sit up and listen carefully.

Some preachers leave all the applications to the very end of the sermon. That is a grave mistake. It assumes that people will remain interested in the sermon until the end. Sadly, that is often not the case, especially when people cannot sense that the sermon is relevant to them. Without application the sermon is like a lecture and the preacher is as boring as the average lecturer. You must apply each sub-point to your hearers and then have a final application at the end of the sermon. How to do this is something you need to continue learning from others and also from reading books on preaching.

Modulating Your Voice and Gestures

In order to preach well you need to pay attention not only to your sermon preparation but also to how you deliver it, that is, the way in which you present your message. This is a very important aspect of preaching and sets it apart from teaching and lecturing. To improve your skills in sermon delivery, you will need to learn how to use your voice and gestures. These are vehicles that communicate not only your ideas but also what those ideas mean to you. They convey your intensity – or your lack thereof. Our goal must be to be like Apollos who "spoke with great fervour and taught about Jesus accurately" (Acts 18:25).

Good preaching is emotional. This is because preachers must first be gripped by the Word of God before they can pass that Word on to their hearers. A preacher is not like a pipe that delivers a liquid from one end to the other without being affected by its contents. Rather, a preacher is like the trunk of a tree, which is nourished by the nutrients from the soil that pass through it on their way to the branches and leaves. Integrity in preaching demands that a preacher must feel what is being spoken about and communicate that to the hearers. So when the passage being expounded is full of joy, the preacher's voice and face will show joy. When the passage being explained is about sin and God's wrath, there will be sadness and seriousness in the voice and on the face of the preacher. That is preaching.

Studying how to preach well means that you learn to use both your voice and your gestures to help you convey God's truth rather than distracting your hearers from it. Your voice and gestures should be as natural as possible. So you must not add brackets in your sermon notes saying "weep here" or "smile here." Your weeping and smiling must flow from the truth you are teaching.

Having said that, you must also continue to ask yourself how much your voice and gestures really represent what you are saying. You should read and think about this as you listen to other preachers, especially preachers who are very effective in their preaching. You will continue to see areas where you can improve. For instance, you may discover that you shout too much or are unnecessarily loud, and so you will have to work to regulate your volume. Or you may discover that you speak in a monotone and need to modulate your voice. Or you may notice that you hold onto the pulpit or keep your hands in your pockets too much, instead of using your hands to help make your points. Paying attention to your voice and your gestures will greatly enhance your effectiveness as a preacher.

Maintaining Eye Contact

Another important aspect of sermon delivery is eye contact. Most of us preachers write out our sermons and take the notes into the pulpit. Sometimes, we can be so concerned with communicating what we have written down that our eyes are more fixed on the notes than on the audience. That can be a distraction because when people notice that we are not looking at them, they tend to feel that we are not addressing them and so their minds wander off to other things. This habit needs to be addressed before we lose our hearers.

As a preacher you need to strike a balance between looking at your notes and looking at your audience. You need to look at your notes sufficiently for you to deliver what you prepared, but you also need to look at your audience sufficiently for them to feel that you really want to address them. There will always be a tension between these two, which you must manage in the full flight of your sermon delivery. Study how you can do this.

Some preachers have photographic memories and can preach a whole sermon without even looking at their notes. Such preachers are few and far between. Most of us lesser mortals need to keep peeping at our notes in order to keep on track. Find a method that will be comfortable for you as you seek to keep a healthy balance between looking at your notes and looking at your audience. One thing is sure; we must all work towards having more eye contact with our audience as far as it is possible.

Stuart Olyott's book *Preaching Pure and Simple*[1] is very helpful on the subject of eye contact. There are many other books that deal with this and the other areas covered in this chapter. Take time to read some of them and apply their lessons to your own preaching.

Discussion Questions

1. What means do you find useful for improving your mastery of the language in which you preach?

2. What other areas do you think preachers should be thinking about as they study how to preach well?

3. Share some of the areas that you have had to work on in your own preaching as you have read books on preaching or listened to other preachers.

4. It can be very hard to come up with good introductions and conclusions. How can you help a pastor who is struggling to improve in these two areas?

---

1. Welwyn Garden City, Herts, UK: Evangelical Press, 2005.

12

Practising Double Listening

I could never be a linesman in football. I cannot imagine how they manage to keep an eye on the players with the ball and also on the players nearest the goal so that they can blow the whistle if someone is offside.[1] When I watch a game, I find it hard to look away from the activities where the ball is – where all the fun and excitement are – and look to see where other are standing.

What I cannot do in football is, however, what pastoral preachers are called to do in real life, that is, to keep their eyes on two places at once. We preachers must keep our eyes on the Bible and on the world. We must be students of both the biblical world and the world in which we and our congregation live. This is because one of the greatest tasks of pastoral preachers is to bring the truths of the Bible to bear upon the lives of God's people in real time. Our hearers must sense that the Bible, which was written thousands of years ago, is relevant to their lives today.

John Stott was making much the same point when he called on pastors to engage in "double listening." A pastoral preacher must have one ear tuned to the Word of God and the other ear to the world of the congregation. This is one of the greatest challenges of being a pastoral preacher, and very few do it well. Some pastors tend to increase their hearers' knowledge of the Bible while failing to show how biblical truths are to be applied in everyday life. Other pastors tend to use the text they read at the start of their sermon as little more than a springboard from which they dive straight into the pool of current affairs, and often there is very little relationship between the text and

---

1. A player is "offside" if someone kicks a ball to them when they are behind all the defenders on the opposing team, except the goalkeeper. The purpose of this rule is to discourage members of the attacking team from lurking near the opposing team's goal rather than being involved in the action.

what they are talking about. In both of these cases, the pastors are failing in the task of "double listening."

Double listening is important not only as regards how we preach but also in regard to what we preach. It will help you to know what passage or passages to preach from so that your sermons are relevant to your people. Young pastors often ask, "How do you find the passage of Scripture to preach from?" That question will be answered if you become a student of the Word and the world.

Being a Student of the Word

Pastoral preachers must be students of the Word of God. It is our primary tool and so it only makes sense for us to be continually learning more about it. So we must read the Bible often and keep growing in our knowledge of its contents from Genesis to Revelation – all sixty-six books. There is more to the Bible than meets the eye, and it is the responsibility of pastors to dig deeper into the Bible so that they see a little more than is obvious to the average reader.

Be a student of the words of the Bible: The Bible was written mainly in two languages – the Old Testament was largely written in Hebrew while the New Testament was largely written in Greek. Very few of us can read it in either of those languages. So much work has been done to convert it into languages we can understand. It is good to keep this in mind because translators are only human, and when you go from one language to another you will invariably lose something. For instance, as I mentioned earlier, the New Testament has different Greek words that are all translated as "love" in our English Bibles. If you are not aware of what word has been used in the Greek, you can easily put the wrong emphasis on what God is saying in the text you are preaching on.

Some of the words of the Bible are "technical" words. That is, they have very specific meanings in the biblical context that are different from their meanings in everyday speech. Think of the word "justification." Today, we use it in sentences like "what justification did they offer for their behaviour?", where "justification" means something like "explanation for why something happened." In the Bible, the word is used quite differently, for it includes a strong element of forgiveness, which is not present in the ordinary use of the word.

There are many other words that are used in special ways when talking about the Christian faith. Think of words like holiness, righteousness, redemption, atonement, propitiation, regeneration, repentance, salvation, adoption, sanctification, glorification, mystery, and so on. Pastor should study these words in their biblical context and understand their full meaning so that they can give their congregations an accurate understanding of the gospel.

The words of the Bible may also have different meanings in different contexts. For instance, the word "law" in the book of Romans sometimes refers to the commandments of God (Rom 7:7–12) and sometimes it refers to something that is more like the law of gravity, in that it is a power or force in our hearts that makes us do things (Rom 7:21, 8:2). Sometimes the word is even used with both meanings in the same sentence (Rom 7:23)! This can be very confusing. Look also at the name Rahab in the Old Testament. We think of Rahab as the woman who hid Joshua's spies and so was rescued from destruction. But then in Job 26:12 we read that "God shattered Rahab" and in Isaiah 51:9 we are told that God "cut Rahab in pieces." What is going on? Did God break his promise? Did Rahab sin in some way and get punished later? Or is the same name being used to refer to different things in the story of Joshua and the poetry of the psalms and the prophets?

Then there are the metaphors of the Bible. For example, the Bible sometimes uses human terms when speaking about God. So it speaks of "the arm of the LORD" (Isa 59:1) as if God has a physical body. Sometimes it speaks as though non-personal things function like persons. For instance, Jesus said that we should let tomorrow worry about itself (Matt 6:34) – as if a day ever worries! The parables of our Lord Jesus Christ are also metaphorical, for he often began them by saying "The kingdom of heaven is like . . ."

Clearly, if you are to be a pastoral preacher you need to grow in your understanding of biblical words and how they are used. And not just the words either. Sometimes, we need to understand something about different genres of writing. Most of us can understand the narrative parts of the Bible, but what about the poetic parts? Hebrew poetry is not the same as English poetry or traditional Zulu poetry. It has its own rules of composition. If you know something about these rules, it will help you bring out the richness of the poetry in the Bible and apply it to your congregation. The same is true of prophetic writing and apocalyptic writing.

Be a student of the history and geography of the Bible: Each of the books of the Bible was written at a specific time in history. It is important for us to know about those times if we are to really appreciate what was being said and written.

Bible history spans thousands of years. Moses, who wrote the first five books of the Bible lived more than 1,000 years before John, who wrote the last book. So we should not be surprised that the Bible mentions a number of political powers, including Egypt, Assyria, Babylon, Persia, Greece and Rome. Having a working knowledge of the circumstances of those nations and empires and their rulers gives you a deeper appreciation of what was going on "behind the scenes," causing all the drama that is recorded in the Bible.

Knowing what was happening at the various times in history and the reasons why the authors of the various books of the Bible wrote what they wrote enables you to apply the text to your current hearers in a way that is truly faithful. For instance, simply knowing that Paul's most joy-filled letter, the one he wrote to the Philippians, was written from prison, gives it added meaning. It makes you want to talk about how Christian joy defies the circumstances in which we find ourselves!

Also, knowing the geography of the places mentioned in the Bible enriches your appreciation of what you are reading. Add to this knowledge about the religious beliefs of the people and the nations referred to in the Bible, and your understanding of what was motivating people to do what they were doing will be deepened.

Be a student of the culture of the Bible: Then there is the issue of the culture of the people in the Bible. Culture is a blind spot. We do not realize how often we impose our own cultural understanding upon the Bible passages we read. For instance, when we read in Deuteronomy 22:5 that a woman must not wear men's clothing nor should a man wear women's clothing, we can easily conclude that it is teaching that women should not wear trousers. In the culture in which this text was being written, men did not wear trousers. They wore robes!

Understanding the cultural context in which the books of the Bible were written also helps us as pastors to know whether something that is taught in the passage is a principle that can be applied or a command that must be obeyed. For instance, Jesus told his disciples in Luke 10:4 not to take a purse or bag or sandals when they went out to evangelize. He even told them not to greet anyone on the way. The Apostle Paul ended a few of his letters with the injunction that believers should greet one another with a holy kiss (1 Cor 16:20). Are these principles to be applied or commands to be obeyed today?

A growing knowledge of the cultural context will help us avoid wrongly applying these texts to the people of God.

Be a student of the redemptive narrative of the Bible: Closely connected to the history of the Bible is its redemptive narrative that runs from Genesis to Revelation. This is the history that overshadows the human history in the Bible. Its heroes are not individuals like Aristotle, Socrates, Plato, Alexander the Great, Julius Caesar, and so on, although these men lived in Bible times. Rather, its heroes are men like Abraham, Joseph, Moses, David, Solomon, and Jesus and his apostles. That is because the story of redemption is at the heart of this redemptive narrative.

The very way the Bible narrative is structured makes it plain that redemption is at its heart. It begins with creation and the fall, and it ends with heaven and glory. It starts with the entry of sin into the world and it ends with the final defeat of sin. The Old Testament prepares us for the coming of the Redeemer, the Lord Jesus Christ, and the New Testament tells us about his coming and the fruit of his life and death. Reading each book of the Bible in the light of its contribution to this great redemptive narrative is a real eye-opener. You feel as if you are watching a great drama unfolding, and the Bible really comes alive. Being conscious of this helps you know how to interpret and apply the Scriptures in a redemptive way to the people of God.

Listening to the World

As you grow in your understanding of the Bible, you must also grow in your understanding of the world in which your hearers live. Both are equally important. Remember, you are not a Bible college lecturer. You are a pastor – a shepherd – of people who are worrying about situations in their lives and undergoing all kinds of trials and temptations. They come to church because they want to hear God speaking clearly into those circumstances. That will happen only as you learn to make biblical teaching relevant to the world in which they live.

Be a student of current affairs: Your people are being affected by the social, political and economic changes taking place all around them. Some of those changes are in the immediate community, others are at a national level, while others are at a global level. Jesus spoke of wars and of rumours of wars (Matt 24:6). These may be happening in places near you or far away, but they cause ripples (or even tsunamis) that reach your people and have an impact on their lives. Your congregation want to know how to live in the light of what is happening.

In rural Africa, your source of information may simply be the local market or a battery-powered radio. If you are closer to a main town or city you may also have access to the local newspapers, though they may be stale by a day or two. Do not underestimate the importance of having your ears in such places. You need to know what is happening around you so that your sermons can be relevant.

In urban Africa, your sources of information are much broader than local gossip and radio. All the modern media are widely available – radio, cable television, newspapers, magazines, the Internet, and so on. Although you must be careful not to spend so much time engrossed in these that you neglect your study of the Bible and your social life, you must not neglect them either. They are essential if you are to appreciate what is happening around you and around your congregation.

Being a student of current affairs means more than knowing what is happening, it also involves thinking deeply about it. It involves asking hard questions: Why is there so much crime or corruption or prostitution in our society? Why are Arabs and Jews failing to get along? Why is Islam causing so much heartache and pain around us? Why is Africa still so underdeveloped? How can we live as God's people in such circumstances? What can we do to stem the tide of evil in our own generation? It is hard thinking about such issues and finding the links between them and the truths of the Bible that produces a true pastor.

Be a student of your own culture: Closely connected to the sphere of current affairs is the area of culture. What do I mean by culture? It is the way in which people generally act or think in a given community or society. Some of it is very positive and commendable, but some of it is negative and unwholesome. The Apostle Paul wrote to Titus about the people in Crete, saying, "One of the Cretans, a prophet of their own, said, 'Cretans are always liars, evil beasts, lazy gluttons.' This testimony is true" (Titus 1:12–13). That was a statement about the culture of the Cretans.

An obvious negative cultural truth about us Africans is that we are not punctual. We are poor timekeepers. That does not mean that every African is poor at timekeeping, but it is generally true of us as a people. As a result, it is very difficult for us to plan communal activities. On the other hand, a more positive cultural reality is that we love singing. We sing when someone is born, we sing when we work, we sing when we play, we sing when we marry, and we sing when someone dies. That is deeply ingrained in our culture.

Culture is also never static. It is dynamic. The way our great-grandparents thought and acted is not the way in which our children think and act. For most of us in urban Africa, Western culture is changing our way of thinking and doing things much more than we would like to admit. What we watch on television and in videos soon leaps out of our screens and walks on two feet in our neighbourhood. Our very music is now so Westernized that if our great-grandparents were to come back from the dead, they would tell us that our current music is totally foreign to our culture. So, although understanding traditional African culture is important, studying culture involves studying how we are behaving today in our society.

The importance of studying culture is that it helps you to understand the worldview behind the thoughts and actions of the people to whom you are ministering. It answers the "why" question and enables you to recognize the hidden idols. Why do we treat wives as if they are a man's property? Why are churches with choirs full to overflowing while those without choirs struggle to survive? Why is the deliverance movement suddenly sweeping across Africa like wildfire? Are the answers to these questions not largely related to our African culture?

Whereas studying current affairs is easy, studying culture is not. A fish is not conscious of the water in which it swims because that is all it knows. Similarly, we take our own culture for granted until an outsider asks us a question about it, or we visit people in another culture and start wondering why they do what they do. That is when we also say, "Come to think of it, why do we do what we do?"

It takes conscious effort to be a student of your own culture. Yet, it is important because only as you address cultural issues will you be challenging God's people to be transformed in their thinking and in their lives (Rom 12:1–2).

Be a student of the human heart: Being a student of the world is basically being a student of the human heart. Ultimately, the current affairs and cultural issues you observe around you are reflections of the condition of the human heart. If you fail to see that you will fail miserably as a pastoral preacher. You will be trying to change people on the outside while their hearts are still in rebellion against God. This will only produce hypocrites, not true followers of Jesus Christ.

The Lord Jesus once said, "What comes out of the mouth proceeds from the heart, and this defiles a person. For out of the heart come evil thoughts, murder, adultery, sexual immorality, theft, false witness, slander" (Matt 15:18–19). Therefore, as a pastoral preacher you should be like a doctor who looks at a patient's symptoms and seeks to diagnose the root cause of the disease. You should not simply notice that there is a lot of deceit in your society or that your culture involves a lot of hypocrisy and then tell the people in your church to be honest. You should go further and recognize that the human heart is fallen and needs to be transformed by the power of the Holy Spirit through Jesus' work of redemption. You will implore your hearers to go to the Lord Jesus Christ, the Great Physician, that he may cure their hearts.

It is in studying the human heart that you will finally find the Bible to be relevant to the people who listen to you, their pastor, every week. Whereas the history and culture of the people in the Bible may be different from ours, their fallen hearts were exactly the same as ours are today. Their hearts betrayed their sinfulness in Bible times in precisely the same way that our hearts do today. Thus, as you explain the Bible to your hearers you will be able to make the bridge from Bible times to today. You will show them themselves in the mirror of Scripture, and then point them to the Saviour for the ultimate cure. In this way you will wonderfully combine the two areas of your double listening because you will bring the real world of Bible times to bear upon the real world of the people in your congregation. This is very demanding, but it is also very rewarding. It will enable you to build a people for God in your generation despite the spiritual darkness that surrounds them.

I mentioned at the start of this chapter that many young pastors ask the question, "How do you find the passage of Scripture to preach from?" I trust that this question has now been answered. Your decision about which passage to use is a fruit of your being immersed in the Word and in the world, and it is an ongoing process. As a pastor, your ongoing Bible study and your knowledge of the world around you will often lead you to books of the Bible or sections of books that will speak to the needs of the people of God at that time. It is as if those books or sections of the Bible will be tugging at you saying, "Preach me!" You will see their relevance and will be persuaded that you owe it to your people to teach them from those passages of Scripture.

Lastly, this "double listening" will also help you to avoid preaching over the heads of your congregation. Your preaching will have hands and feet. It will touch the lives of your people and it will seem to walk where they are walking. It will be clothed in language they understand and will have applications that are relevant to the here and now in their lives. This is a challenge you must face squarely if you are going to be a powerful pastoral preacher. "Double listening" will make you a potent weapon in the hands of God.

Discussion Questions

1. How can we as pastors in a common neighbourhood share books or information on useful Web sites to help one another in our preaching?

2. What news channels do you find most informative and useful to enable you to make intelligent references to current affairs in your sermons?

3. What are the most common challenges in your community among different groups of people (young and old, men and women, rich and poor, churched and un-churched, etc.) and what does the Bible say about these challenges?

4. What practical steps can you take to ensure that you are getting honest feedback from your congregation to show that you are not preaching over their heads?

Section E

Using the Whole Bible in Pastoral Preaching

13

Preaching from Narrative Passages

Africans love stories. A day in an African village ends with stories, when the evening meal is over and the children gather around the fire to listen to the family storyteller. As the sparks from the flames rise into the evening sky, the imagination of the hearers is captured by the skilful narration of folktales. Tension develops as the plot unfolds. All is finally resolved as the people with evil intent are finally defeated and good triumphs.

Even though I grew up in a city, I have vivid memories of such times. My cousin, who was almost my dad's age, would come to visit us about once a year. We looked forward to his coming because each evening he would sit down and say, "Once upon a time . . ." We preferred listening to him to watching television. His stories were closer to life as we knew it, and the lessons learnt were at our level. His stories taught us to obey our parents and respect the elderly. We also learnt the principle of sowing and reaping from this man's annual visits.

Most of the Bible is also written in the form of stories. From Genesis to Job is almost all narrative. Even in the books of the prophets we find stories that give us the context of the prophecies. In the New Testament, the Gospels and the Acts of the Apostles are all narratives. Therefore, if you are going to use the whole Bible as a pastoral preacher in ministering to your people, you will need to learn to preach from narrative passages. Hopefully you will be as skilful as the village storytellers.

Stories about God and His Ways

The stories in the Bible were written largely for a pastoral reason. Their authors were not simply setting out to record historical events but were deliberately choosing stories that would teach the people of God about God and his ways, so that future generations would know how to please him. Therefore, as you read the stories in the Bible and notice the details in them, keep asking yourself, "Why are we being told this?" There is a reason. In finding that reason, you will be on your way to finding out what the author wants you to know about God and his ways.

The Apostle Paul was quite clear about his reasons for referring to stories from the past: "these things took place as examples for us, that we might not desire evil as they did" (1 Cor 10:6). He did not want the Corinthian believers to be ignorant of what had happened to the people of Israel during their journey from Egypt to the promised land. He warned them against idolatry, sexually immorality and testing God by reminding them of Old Testament stories about people who did such things and paid dearly for doing so (vv. 7–10). Then he repeated his point that "these things happened to them as an example, but they were written down for our instruction, on whom the end of the ages has come" (v. 11). The Apostle then went on to tell the Corinthian believers about God's faithfulness and about the fact that God does not allow his people to be tempted beyond their ability (vv.12–13).

God inspired the various individuals who wrote the Bible so that his children across the ages would know him and his ways. The narrative passages play that role particularly well. This is partly we see ourselves in the godly or ungodly characters in the narratives. We see our own sinfulness in the actions of the people in the stories. We become engrossed in the plot, and before we know it, we hear God saying to our consciences, "You are the man!" It is too late then to put up the shield. The arrow is already in the heart and we have to go to him for pardon and grace. That is the power of narratives.

Unlike our village stories, biblical stories are written from God's perspective, and every so often this is made explicit. For instance, in the story of David and Bathsheba, after David had managed to hide his sin from everyone and had already married Bathsheba, the author adds, "But the thing that David had done displeased the LORD" (1 Sam 11:27). That is powerful! It makes us see the ordinary events of our lives from God's perspective. That is important for pastoral preaching because you want to help God's people live their daily lives knowing that God is in control of all things, sees all things, and will deal with us according to the moral choices that we are making.

The biblical narratives also have a redemptive thread running through them. They point us to our need of Christ, they show us the saving life of Christ, and they reveal the kind of lives we ought to live in the light of what Christ has done for us and can do in us by the power of his Spirit. Some of the Old Testament characters are even types or pictures of Christ in a general sense, showing something of his saving work. For example, Melchizedek was a type of Christ because he was both priest and king (Heb 6:20), and Jonah was a type of Christ by being in the belly of the fish for three days and three nights (Matt 12:39–40).

In the New Testament, the Gospel of John made this redemptive purpose very clear: "Now Jesus did many other signs in the presence of the disciples, which are not written in this book; but these are written so that you may believe that Jesus is the Christ, the Son of God, and that by believing you may have life in his name" (John 20:30–31). From the many events that took place in the life of Jesus, most of which John himself witnessed, he chose a few and strung them together with a very clear purpose in mind. It was to help his readers put their trust in Jesus as their Saviour. John had a redemptive goal in his writing, and we must have a redemptive goal when we are preaching through his gospel in order to be true to his writings. All the Scriptures, including the narrative passages, are ultimately about Jesus Christ.

Finding the Start and End of the Story

If you are going to make proper use of the breadth of information in the narrative passages of the Bible, your first task will be to find the start and the end of the particular story from which you are going to preach. This is usually not as easy as simply going from the start of a chapter to the end of that chapter. Sometimes chapters divide narratives in the same way that national boundaries divide many African countries, cutting right through the middle of villages. So, do not depend on the chapter divisions. Do your own homework.

Thankfully, most stories in the Bible have a plot that builds towards a crisis which is later resolved. The start of the story is thus the point where the author begins to build towards the crisis. He may refer to a time when a king was preparing to go to war or a time when a famine started. It is evident that he is setting the scene. Then the characters are mentioned who get the plot into motion. That is probably the start of the story.

What about the end? Usually, it is when the crisis of the plot is resolved. Often it is by the intervention of God, so that he is seen as ever-present and active in human affairs. Stories in the Bible are like a journey up a hill and down the other side. The hilltop is the crisis point. When you have climbed the hill and come down the other side, you can tell that you have arrived. You are back in a valley again.

Finding the Big Idea

In Bible narratives, the author usually has one major lesson about God and his ways that he wants his readers to know through that one story. So, when you have found the start and the end of the story, ask yourself, "What is the major lesson in this story?" In preaching, this is called "the big idea." Usually, the big idea is some theological or redemptive truth. Remember, the Bible is about God and his ways. So, the big idea is likely to be a truth about God or a truth about the ways of God, especially his way of salvation.

The big idea is rarely a good example for us to follow or a bad example for us to avoid. I state this because that is all that many pastors see in biblical narratives. In the end their sermons are nothing more than moralizing. Village stories end with the bad people being defeated through an unexpected turn of events so that young people can learn that it does not pay to be a bad person. The Bible goes far beyond that.

Developing the Big Idea

Once you have found the big idea of the story, your next task as a pastoral preacher is to see how the narrative brings out this big idea. The steps that the author uses to make the big idea stand out in bold relief are the steps you will use in developing your sermon. In short, let the story itself determine the structure of your sermon. There will be rare circumstances when you will think that you need to jumble the story a little in order to make a particular point, but this should not be the norm. The Holy Spirit knows why he inspired the author of the narrative to write in the way that he wrote, and we should follow in the footprints of the Holy Spirit.

Once you have worked out the structure of your sermon using the contours of the story, then it is time to take out your commentaries and other

Bible helps. The commentaries will provide details that help fill out the story you are going to preach on. There is usually some background information that scholars have unearthed that will help you to understand the story even better. Understanding historical and cultural contextual data enriches the plot, and you will feel the excitement of the unfolding events even more. You want to pass this excitement on to your hearers when you preach your sermon, so that they too can get caught up in the drama and feel its impact upon their lives.

Sometimes as you fill in the gaps and develop the big idea, you will find that your sermon grows into two, three, four, or even five sermons. In other words, the big idea breaks down into a number of major lessons and you do not want to rush through them. This often happens when various scenes in the plot have very important lessons that your congregation needs to chew over slowly. You are their pastor. You know their needs. You do not want to simply give counsel "on the run." You want to pull over to the side of the road, switch off the engine, and apply the parking brake for a while. Or, to change the picture, you want to squeeze as much juice from the mango as possible for the health of your people. What should you do?

It is best not to break a story up into different sermons but to present it all at once. However, you may preach from one scene of a story as long as you remain faithful to the overall big idea. For instance, in the story of the Prodigal Son, the main idea is probably the nature of God's grace towards sinners. If you were to preach a sermon about the scene where the younger son demands his share of his father's estate, you might want to focus on the theme of how sinful our hearts are. That will fit into the overall theme because it will magnify the grace of God. On the other hand, if the message you draw from that scene focuses on the father's love in allowing his son to go away, your message will not really contribute to magnifying the grace of God. So, it is possible to have more than one sermon per story, but it must be done carefully so that you do not detract from the big idea.

Four Common Errors to Avoid

There are four major errors to avoid when you are preaching on narrative portions of the Bible. The first is putting more into the story than is actually there. This is often a result of wanting to "juice up" the story so that it becomes more interesting or wanting to say something different from what is really in the text. While there is some legitimate filling in of the gaps to explain Bible narratives, you must be careful not to push the boundary until you make the Bible say what it is not really saying.

For instance, it is legitimate to say that the father in the parable of the Prodigal Son had to pull up his robes as he ran to welcome his son. It certainly captures the imagination and would have been true because people wore robes in those days. However, to add that his wife felt embarrassed to see an old man like him running like that may be saying a little more than Scripture warrants. There is nothing in the text that suggests it was culturally embarrassing for a man to run towards his long lost son.

The second error to avoid is turning the descriptions of the narratives into prescriptions. In other words, we should not assume that we are meant to do exactly the same things that the people in the stories did. Rather, the stories are meant to teach us principles that we must apply in our own context. For example, Nazirites were told not to shave their heads or beards (Num 6:1–5). This does not mean that in order to be consecrated to God men should not shave. Many Old Testament practices are shown in the New Testament to have been signifying something spiritual. Or, to take another example, in the New Testament Jesus went into the mountains to pray. This does not mean that we should all be going to pray in the mountains. The principle we are to learn from this is the importance of solitude - spending time alone with God.

The third error is allegorizing. This is the tendency to give something in a story a meaning that is not warranted by the text of Scripture itself or by another part of the Bible. For instance, simply because of its colour, many interpret the scarlet cord that Rahab tied to her window to stop the Israelites from killing her family as symbolizing the blood of Christ. Others use the story of David killing Goliath to say we must slay giant sins in our hearts. That is allegorizing. We do have at least one example of biblical allegorizing in Galatians 4:22–24:

> For it is written that Abraham had two sons, one by a slave woman and one by a free woman. But the son of the slave was born according to the flesh, while the son of the free woman was born through promise. Now this may be interpreted allegorically: these women are two covenants. One is from Mount Sinai, bearing children for slavery; she is Hagar.

That is legitimate allegorizing because it is warranted by the text of Scripture itself. As a general rule, however, avoid going down this road. The meaning of most narratives is on the surface; you do not need to allegorize.

The fourth error is moralizing. This is the tendency to interpret the text of Scripture only in terms of good examples to follow and bad examples to avoid. We do this when all we say is "Joseph did not take revenge on his brothers, and so we must not take revenge on those who wrong us. David committed adultery with Bathsheba and suffered for it. We must not do what he did." To be sure, that is true. The narrative passages do give us good examples to imitate and bad examples to avoid, but that is not the primary goal of Scripture. After all, in ourselves we do not have the power to live the way we should. We have fallen hearts. God wants us to go deeper than merely trying to copy the people in the Bible or trying to avoid their bad examples. He wants us to see the inner workings of our hearts and turn to Christ as our ultimate healer.

Exposing the Inner Workings of the Heart

In order to make the most of pastoral preaching from narratives, be sure to ask "why" questions during your sermon preparation. Why did he do this? Why did she react that way? It is in seeking answers to these questions that you become a real physician of souls in your preaching. Why did Cain kill Abel? Why did Peninnah mock Hannah? Why did David, who already had more wives than you can care to count, commit adultery with Bathsheba and go on to murder her husband in order to hide his sin? Why did he not own up the moment Bathsheba told him she was pregnant?

You will often find that the answer to these "why" questions takes you to the sinfulness of our human hearts. Cain did not kill Abel because he was bad, whereas we are good. Peninnah did not mock Hannah because she was bad, whereas we are good. David did not commit adultery because he was bad, whereas we are good. They all acted as they did because their hearts were sinful, and our hearts are also sinful. Placed in the same circumstances, we would be prone to act in the same way that they did.

Once pastoral preaching exposes our human hearts, it should point us to "the fountain filled with blood drawn from Emmanuel's veins." It should cause us to resolve to live a life that is pleasing to God and that follows his ways. Recognizing that we do not have the power to do that in our own strength, pastoral preaching should point us to Christ as the one who saves and sanctifies his people. He alone is able to cure the human heart from its sinfulness.

Moralizing biblical narratives turns your congregation into an assembly of hypocrites. Pointing your congregation to the Saviour through these narratives turns them into truly godly men and women, because when they come to Christ he not only washes their sins away by his blood, but he also causes his Spirit to positively transform their hearts.

Narrative preaching is glorious once you know how to do it well:

> Preaching narratives is a delight. Finding the main idea of the story is a mysterious adventure that results in a wonderful climax. Leading a congregation through disequilibrium is also a grand adventure. Watching people go through an "aha" experience as the sermon plot is revealed is awesome. Finally, leading them to resolutions that are real, because they are based on true narratives, is genuinely satisfying. You will preach ideas you never thought the Bible articulated. And as a result, you will see congregations make choices that are astounding.[1]

Discussion Questions

1. Recall one or two stories you were told in your childhood that had a great impact on you. Why do you think those stories left such a deep impression?

2. What are some of the wrong ways in which preachers find Christ in the narrative passages of the Bible?

3. Apart from the four common errors mentioned in this chapter, do you know of any other errors that preachers should avoid when preaching from narrative passages of the Bible?

4. Name a few Old Testament characters other than Melchizedek and Jonah who are types or pictures of Christ and explain how they represent Christ.

---

1. Paul Borden and Steven D. Matthewson, eds., "The Big Idea of Narrative Preaching" in Haddon Robinson and Craig Brian in *The Art and Craft of Biblical Preaching: A Comprehensive Resource for Today's Communicators* (Grand Rapids, MI: Zondervan, 2016). Also available online at www.preachingtoday.com/skills/2005/august/73--borden.html

14

Preaching from Didactic Passages

The Bible is a very rich book. It has narrative passages that young children can understand, but it also has passages that are more abstract and demand a little more maturity to process. As pastors we are to use all parts and genres of the Bible for the instruction of the people of God. As Paul said to Timothy, "All Scripture is breathed out by God and profitable for teaching, for reproof, for correction, and for training in righteousness, that the man of God may be complete, equipped for every good work" (2 Tim 3:16–17). So the whole Bible is given to us for use in building up of the body of Christ. That is not as easy as it sounds because some parts are easier to preach from than others. Hence the Apostle Paul exhorts Timothy, "Do your best to present yourself to God as one approved, a worker who has no need to be ashamed, rightly handling the word of truth" (2 Tim 2:15). We must learn to handle and preach from every part of the Word of God in the right way.

We have looked at how to preach correctly from narrative passages; now let us turn to preaching correctly from didactic passages. This chapter is not meant to provide comprehensive information on how to prepare expository sermons on didactic passages of the Bible. There are other books that deal with that. My goal is simply to provide pointers so that someone who is involved in pastoral preaching will appreciate the extra tools God has given us in the didactic passages as we seek to build a people for God.

Didactic Passages Teach about God Directly

As a pastor, one of your greatest responsibilities is to ground God's people in the truths of the Christian faith. In an earlier chapter I said that Christians need to develop a biblical view of God, creation, human beings, history, sin, redemption in Christ, salvation applied by the Holy Spirit, the church, the state, missions, the second coming of Christ, and so on. While this can be done through preaching from narrative passages, the primary sources of doctrinal instruction are the didactic passages in the Bible. These are passages that are clearly intended to teach and instruct. That is why they often use the word "you" as the author addresses the readers directly. He argues his case and applies the truths to his readers.

The main didactic passages in the Bible are found in the Epistles (or Letters), which comprise twenty-one out of the twenty-seven books of the New Testament. That is enough material to keep any pastor occupied for many years as he instructs God's people! There are also other less obvious didactic passages, such as the sermons in the Gospels and in the Acts of the Apostles. Our Lord's Sermon on the Mount, for example, is a didactic passage. Even some of the Lord's discourses with people he met are didactic simply because he was teaching wherever he went. The most famous verse in the whole Bible, John 3:16, was uttered while he was talking with Nicodemus. The Lord Jesus was teaching Nicodemus about God, and in that sense it is a didactic passage and must be preached as such. In didactic passages truths about God and his ways are stated and applied in the text itself. As a pastor, all you need to do is proclaim the truths that are lying on the very surface of the text to your congregation.

Take an important doctrinal subject like justification. It is a topic that every Christian must understand if they are not to spend many years in a spiritual wilderness being buffeted by Satan. Yet it is a very difficult topic to teach using narrative passages because the concept is highly technical. So the best way to teach it is to use passages that are deliberately teaching passages. Chapters 3 to 5 of the book of Romans, for example, contain enough didactic material to thoroughly instruct a congregation in this all-important subject. By the time you get to the end of chapter 5, your congregation will be resting squarely on the impregnable rock of justification by faith alone. That is the importance of didactic passages.

Finding the Expository Unit

When preparing to preach from a narrative passage, you start by finding the beginning and the end of a story. When you want to preach from a didactic passage, you begin by finding an expository unit. An expository unit is a section of a passage that contains one major thought. Quite often you will find that a paragraph constitutes an expository unit (after all, a paragraph is defined as a distinct section dealing with a single line of thought). When authors sense that they have exhausted what they wanted to state about one idea, or when Bible translators conclude that an author's line of thought has come to an end, they tend to start another paragraph. So, this is the best way to divide expository units. Of course, this rule cannot be set in concrete because sometimes the expository unit overflows into other paragraphs. It is simply a good place to start as a general rule.

Once you have found the expository unit, your next task is to understand the passage itself. Listen very carefully to its logic. Like a miner, you must follow the vein of the ore in order to extract the mineral successfully. Take note of the connecting words and phrases ("and," "but," "for," "because," "therefore," "so then," and so on) and you will soon see the logical flow of the passage. Your goal is to finally arrive at "the big idea" of the text as you see the way in which its connecting words bring out its meaning. You want to reach a point where you can say in one sentence what the whole passage is about. That is "the big idea" of the text and it will determine the main thrust of your sermon.

While doing this, it is also important to bear in mind the style of the author. The Apostle John, for instance, writes in a more circular style than the Apostle Paul, whose arguments are usually more linear.

Digging Deeper into the Didactic Passage

You will find it helpful to dig deeper into the didactic passage you will be preaching from. Not everything that you will learn about the passage will be communicated to your congregation, but your study will certainly increase your appreciation of the text.

Begin with its literary context. See what the passages before and after your expository unit are saying, so that you understand the larger flow in which it is found. Then go on to investigate the historical context. Try to find out more about the events that led to the writing of this passage, the circumstances of the author, the people to whom he was writing, and so on. Knowing this background enriches your understanding of the text and will enrich your preaching on it. You may sometimes find it helpful to mention the circumstance in which the passage was written in the introduction to your sermon. These same circumstances may also help you apply your sermon.

Pay attention to the exact words that convey the message of the text. Look for the long words, the repeated words, the unusual words, and the significant words. Make use of a Bible dictionary as you try to understand exactly what each word means. Compare the translations of this passage in a few Bible versions as well. Variations in the translations should alert you to the need to look more closely at the words in the text. These types of word studies are particularly important when it comes to didactic passages because a wrong understanding of one word can lead to an incorrect interpretation of the whole passage and wrong application of the sermon.

You should also consult one or two reliable commentaries. They are very handy in establishing the circumstances in which the passage was written and also in explaining some of the difficulties in the text. Let's face it, some didactic passages are very difficult to understand. As a pastor, you do not want to teach something you will later need to correct. So you want to ensure that you understand the passage correctly before you go into the pulpit.

Once you have dug deep into the text and have reduced the passage to one statement, you are ready to move into sermon construction:

> Only when one is able to trace the actual way in which the argument develops within a paragraph has the text been understood well enough to preach it. . . . Preaching in the Epistles means to construct a sermon which is faithful to the author's original intention as expressed in the various assertions in the text in their original context, which is first and foremost the literary context of the argument in which they "live and move and have their being."[1]

Constructing a Sermon from a Didactic Passage

When dealing with a didactic passage, you must use "the big idea" of the text to form "the big idea" of the sermon. In other words, you must go from a summary of what the passage was teaching the people at the time it was written to a summary of what the passage should teach the people in your church. The message must be the same, but your job is to bridge the gap of time and clothe that same teaching from the Bible with twenty-first century clothing so that it will be relevant to God's people today. The Holy Spirit wants

---

1. Scott Hafemann, "Preaching in the Epistles," in *Handbook of Contemporary Preaching*, ed. Michael Duduit (Nashville, TN: Broadman and Holman, 1992), 364.

to speak the same truths to your hearers that he taught the people in Bible days. After all, they are all God's people – why should they have a different set of truths?

Once you are clear about the content of "the big idea" for your hearers, you must seek clarity as to what you hope it will achieve in their lives. You must not only teach the truths that are being taught in the didactic passage but must also seek to achieve the same moral and spiritual goals that the original author was seeking to achieve in the lives of his hearers. Like a doctor taking a patient's pulse, you must feel the pulse of the author if you are to convey something about his heart to your hearers. This must be the goal or purpose of your sermon, and it will shape the applications of your sermon.

The structure of your sermon must, as far as possible, reflect the structure of the text. The logic in the text will then be the logic in the sermon. This will help your hearers to grow in their understanding of the Bible, and when they read the passage later on their own, it will be full of light. When your logic follows the logic of the text, your application tends to carry with it the weight of the text and its impact is unforgettable. Your hearers sense that this is not their pastor talking to them. You are simply a conduit through whom the Word of God is coming to them with new understanding and fresh application. They can see the truth in the text and they can also feel its weight in their hearts.

Making Sermons from Didactic Passages Captivating

One advantage of preaching from narrative passages is that the text itself captures the attention and engages the imagination of your hearers. Stories always have that effect, which is why we love them. With didactic passages, however, the sermon can easily become dry and boring. If you are not very careful, you may fail to connect with your hearers. As a pastoral preacher who is preaching through an epistle, for example, you must work doubly hard to capture the attention of your congregation and then keep their interest to the very end. How do you do that?

The answer is that you need to take seriously what was said in chapter 11 about how to preach well. Whether you have taken to heart the challenges given in that chapter will be seen primarily in how you handle didactic passages. If you master the use of words, have arresting introductions, structure the body of your sermon so that it progresses in a straight line, and deliver conclusions that grip the heart, you will find your people coming back for more sermons based on didactic passages. As you learn to use relevant illustrations and applications, your congregation will feel that you are talking to them in their world. Through good use of your voice and gestures you will hold their attention as you take them through even the most difficult didactic passages. And, finally, as you look them in the eyes, rather than always looking at your notes, they will think you are really interested in them and will keep following what you are saying. There is no new magic bullet, just the same ground we have already covered. Learn how to preach well and it will show as you expound didactic passages as a pastoral preacher.

Discussion Questions

1. In many places around the world, it is very rare for preachers to expound didactic passages. They simply use them as starting points for topical sermons. Why do you think this is so?

2. What do you think congregations lose if they hear only narrative or topical sermons and rarely hear faithful expository sermons based on didactic passages?

3. Listen to or read a sermon on a didactic passage and identify the passage, the word studies, the context, etc., and how the preacher uses them.

4. Preaching from didactic passages can be dry and boring to many listeners. What have you found helpful to legitimately liven up such sermons?

15

Preaching from Poetic and Prophetic Passages

Charles Haddon Spurgeon once said that when preachers get tired of preaching the gospel they turn to preaching on prophecy instead. He was not far from the truth. If the danger of preaching from narrative passages is moralizing and the danger of preaching from didactic passages is giving a dry and boring presentation, then the danger of preaching from poetic and prophetic passages is teaching heresy. So many cults have been spawned from the prophetic passages of the Bible that we cannot be too careful. We need to take extra care as we preach such passages to our congregations.

Having said that, it must also be said that poetic and prophetic passages are the most neglected parts of the Bible. This is as true for the individual in the pew as it is for the pastor in the pulpit. And yet poetic and prophetic passages comprise one-third of the Bible. So in neglecting these passages we are depriving God's people of an important part of God's holy Word. This situation needs to be reversed so that our pastoral preaching becomes more balanced and comprehensive.

One major reason for this neglect is the fact that the poetic and prophetic sections of the Bible are harder to interpret than narrative and didactic portions. Anyone who has attempted to study or preach faithfully from those portions of the Bible will agree. Preaching from these passages demands a lot more time for preparation, and since time is a scarce commodity for pastors, the inevitable happens – the poetic and prophetic passages are neglected. So my goal in this chapter is not so much to give you a general idea of how to preach from the poetic and prophetic passages but rather to demystify those passages and give you sufficient reason to preach from them. Other authors have written in more detail on how to preach from these passages.

Poetic and Prophetic Passages of the Bible

Which books of the Bible are poetic and prophetic? The poetic books are those from Job onwards, up to the end of the Old Testament. They include most of the prophetic books. The prophetic books are the Major (or longer) Prophets – Isaiah, Jeremiah, Lamentations, Ezekiel, and Daniel – and the Minor (or shorter) Prophets – the twelve books from Hosea to the end of the Old Testament. This category accounts for quite a significant chunk of the Bible – twenty-two of the sixty-six books, including, the longest book in the Bible, Jeremiah. You can see how we impoverish the people of God and ourselves when we neglect such a large portion of the Scriptures.

Handling the Poetic Passages

Let us begin with the poetic passages. Poetry is a style of writing used to express personal thoughts and emotions. It often has an element of rhythm, which is why poems are often set to music. The divinely inspired hymnbook of the Bible – the book of Psalms – is written as poetry.

It is striking that God decided to reveal himself to us not only in prose but also in poetry. That tells us something about the kind of God we worship. He knows we are not only intellectual creatures but are also emotional and artistic. It is remarkable that some of the most scathing messages penned by his prophets took the form of poetry!

Poets everywhere tend to use rich imagery and figures of speech to express themselves, and biblical poets are no exception. They use the idea of trees clapping their hands to express excitement. They speak about mountains being uprooted and cast into the sea when they want to describe calamity and commotion. They speak about being led to green pastures and quiet waters that represent satisfaction and fulfilment. When interpreting poetic passages you must be careful not to interpret such expressions literally, otherwise you will arrive at some very absurd conclusions.

Preaching from poetic passages will help your congregation to realize how personal and intense their walk with God can be, because the poets express a wide variety of emotions. The book of Job shows the intensity of a man's suffering despite his integrity as he walks with God. The emotions of the psalmists range from desperation and frustration to joyful praise. Even in the book of Proverbs, which is presented in the form of an older person's counsel to someone younger, you sense the speaker's personal involvement in what is being conveyed, especially in the prologues to the counsel (Prov 4:1–9).

The book of Ecclesiastes reveals the frustrations of a child of God as he tries to understand the events of the world around him. The Song of Solomon explores the emotions of marital love, which is God's gift to humankind and to his church. Poetry certainly reaches places in our hearts that other forms of literature do not.

Yet these are not merely emotions. They are emotions that reveal something of the godly person's hunger for God. Job suffered because of his desire to walk with God in integrity. The psalmists pray and praise because of their relationship with God. The counsels of the book of Proverbs are given so that the young can walk in the fear of God, which is the beginning of wisdom. The book of Ecclesiastes works its way through all the frustrations to arrive at the conclusion, "Fear God and keep his commandments, for this is the whole duty of man" (Eccl 12:13). The Song of Solomon rejoices in God's gift of marriage, which ultimately points to the relationship between Jesus and the church. Preaching pastorally through these poetic books enriches the lives of believers as they see their own desire for God expressed by and augmented in these poetic writings.

These poetic passages also point to Christ, who said, "These are my words that I spoke to you while I was still with you, that everything written about me in the Law of Moses and the Prophets and the Psalms must be fulfilled" (Luke 24:44). Some psalms point to Christ directly and are what we call messianic psalms. Other poetic passages point to him more indirectly. It is vital to learn how to relate these passages to Christ in your pastoral preaching in a way that does not lead you down the slippery path of allegory.

Hebrew poetry has a lot in common with English poetry, but it also has its own unique features. English poetry emphasizes rhyming and metre while Hebrew poetry emphasizes what we call parallelism. In other words, Hebrew poets repeat a line in different ways to give it a "stereo" effect that enhances our awareness of what is being said. Understanding this feature of Hebrew poetry can help you avoid a common cause of wrong interpretations and applications.

Let me give you examples of the three basic types of Hebrew parallelism from Isaiah 53.

Synonymous parallelism, in which the second line repeats and reinforces the first.

> He had no form or majesty that we should look at him,
> and no beauty that we should desire him" (Isa 53:2b).

Synthetic parallelism, in which the second line elaborates on the thought of the first.

> Yet we esteemed him stricken,
> smitten by God, and afflicted (Isa 53:4b).

Antithetic parallelism, in which the second line contrasts with the thought of the first.

> He was oppressed, and he was afflicted,
> yet he opened not his mouth (Isa 53:7).

You need to become familiar with these poetic forms and their rules of composition. Knowing them will not only help you to understand what the poets were saying to their first hearers but will also help you to communicate that message to your congregation as you preach on a poetic passage.

There will always be difficulties in interpreting some poetic passages, which will demand a lot more work of you. For instance, the imprecatory psalms are tough to handle in an age of worldwide grace after Pentecost. These psalms call on God to judge or destroy or bring calamity upon God's enemies or wicked people. And yet we still need to preach on passages like Psalm 69:24–28 and Psalm 109 because they are part of "all Scripture," which is God-breathed and useful for the instruction of the people of God.

Handling the Prophetic Passages

Let us now turn to the prophetic passages. The name "prophetic" can be misleading because we tend to think of prophecy as involving the foretelling of future events. Although the prophets had that ability and even foretold the first and second coming of Christ, most of their messages were directed to their own people, condemning them for violating their covenant obligations and calling them to repentance. Therefore, they offer ready-made sermons that you may simply adapt and preach in the context of your pastoral ministry.

When preaching from the prophetic passages, it is important for you to know roughly when the prophets wrote their books, who their contemporaries were, and their primary audience. Do not make the mistake of assuming that the books are arranged in chronological order in the Bible. Nor should you assume that the Major Prophets spoke to only one nation. In fact, their books are often collections of prophecies addressed to various nations.

One of the greatest challenges in understanding and preaching from the prophetic books is the historical, geographical, and cultural distance that separates them from us. In one sense, this is true of the narrative and didactic books as well. However, with narrative passages, a lot of historical information is there in the text itself. With didactic passages, the historical context in which they were written may be less important. But the prophetic books leave you wondering what nations and cities had done to warrant such scathing condemnation by the prophets. Why were these peoples being called to repentance? Having this background information makes a world of a difference to your understanding of the prophetic passages you are going to be preaching from. You will then understand what the prophets were saying and why they wrote the things they did.

When studying and preaching from the prophetic books, you must remember that the prophets were convinced that God is sovereign over all the nations and peoples of the earth and that he is faithful to his covenant agreement with his people. Once you are clear about the first point (God's sovereignty) you will begin to understand why he threatens to destroy powerful nations and calls them to repentance through his prophets. He is King of kings and Lord of lords. Also, once you are clear about the second point (God's covenant faithfulness) you will begin to understand why he punishes his people – the nation of Israel – and then tenderly calls them back to himself through the prophets. The sovereignty and faithfulness of God are powerful keys to unlocking the writings of the prophets. They are also powerful keys to preaching pastorally from the prophetic passages.

The prophetic passages also include prophecies about the future. What can we say about such prophecies? First, we can be thankful that most of the future events described in the prophetic passages have already happened. The prophecies relating to the first coming of Christ have been fulfilled to the smallest detail. When we read them, we have the advantage of hindsight, which the first hearers of those prophecies did not. We can preach about such prophecies as both foretold and fulfilled. This goes a long way to giving believers confidence that the Bible is truly inspired by the all-seeing, all-knowing God.

Then there are the prophetic passages which refer to events that have not yet happened. These prophecies are normally related to the second coming of Christ and the period immediately preceding it. You will note that the prophets sometimes speak about the events related to the first and second coming of Christ as if they will happen with only one day between them! The apocalyptic passages in the books of Daniel and Revelation include a number of prophecies related to the second coming of Christ. As a pastor, it is important to preach on those passages, but it is also important to do so with caution. Mishandling of these prophetic passages has given birth to all kinds of cults. So it is unwise to be dogmatic about the exact nature and timing of the fulfilment of future prophecies. The very fact that these passages are clothed in figures of speech suggests that the authors wanted them to remain as general warnings so that we are always ready. That is the emphasis you must take as you preach on them.

Most of the prophetic passages are written in poetic form. This is how God inspired the ancient seers to pen their prophecies. Therefore, it is important to observe the rules of interpretation that are related to poetic passages when studying these passages and preparing sermons from them. Similarly, narrative passages that are written in prose should be handled in accordance with the rules for narrative passages discussed in chapter 13.

Finally, the prophetic passages must also be interpreted with Christ at the centre. Remember the words of Jesus, "These are my words that I spoke to you while I was still with you, that everything written about me in the Law of Moses and the Prophets and the Psalms must be fulfilled" (Luke 24:44). So as you preach from the prophetic writings, keep in mind that they speak about Christ. Instead of pandering to the curiosity of God's people by forcing your own political guesswork into the prophetic passages of Scripture, you should point them to Christ as the one who fulfils all Scripture.

Discussion Questions

1. Why is it that prophetic passages of the Bible have been the springboard of many cults, and what should you do to avoid falling into similar error?

2. In this chapter, you were introduced to the three most basic types of Hebrew parallelism. Read more on this subject and share what other types of parallelism can be found in the Bible, giving examples.

3. Listen to or read a good sermon on a poetic or prophetic passage of the Bible. Note how the preacher explains the figures of speech, the parallelism, etc., and applies it to New Testament believers. What do you learn from this to improve your own preaching?

4. Many of the Old Testament passages Christ quotes as referring to himself come from the poetic or prophetic passages of the Old Testament. Look at one or two such passages and discuss how this enriches your understanding and preaching of those Old Testament chapters.

Section F

Power for Pastoral Preaching

16

The Pastor's Study Life

Many years ago I attended a denominational pastors' retreat where the main speaker was an older man who had already pastored two churches. During a question-and-answer session he was asked how long a pastor should remain in one church. He replied, "No more than five years." Seeing the surprise on our faces, he went on to give his rationale: "You see, it takes about five years for a church to catch up with its pastor's level of knowledge. So, if he does not move on, there will be growing dissatisfaction with his ministry and he will end up being forced out." I was still new in the ministry at that time and this statement struck me forcefully. It left me with a nagging question: "While my church members are growing in their knowledge, shouldn't I also be growing in my knowledge of the things of God?"

There is something to be said for the overall thinking of this older pastor. Pastors do command a certain respect based on their understanding of the Word of God. When congregations perceive that their pastors know more than they do, they eagerly receive the pastors' teaching. The opposite is equally true. Christians get impatient when a pastor's sermons become predictable and they are no longer learning anything new. That is when they conclude it is time to find a new pastor. This is especially true where the congregation includes persons with high levels of education.

Sadly, many pastors think that the best way to sustain their ministry in a church is by playing a power game. They surround themselves with leaders who are "yes" men and have a touch-not-the-Lord's-anointed mentality. They claim to have received some mystical anointing that places them beyond any form of questioning. In Africa, where chiefs rule without being questioned and witch doctors are feared for their mystical powers, it is not surprising that some pastors adopt similar strategies to maintain their positions. Such pastors have a personal-to-holder grip on their churches. Those who feel short-changed are the ones who have to leave the church and go into the wilderness looking for greener pasture. The result is a very high turnover of church members and a failure by pastors to build a people for God.

What should be done to reverse this trend? What is the right kind of power that pastors should have? What is the true source of spiritual authority? It is obviously the Holy Spirit. But what are the means that the Holy Spirit uses to bestow power so that pastors retain freshness over years of preaching ministry? This chapter deals with the first means – the pastor's study life.

Loving God with Your Mind

The primary reason for cultivating a devoted study life is not to have a long pastorate by remaining the church's number one authority on divine matters. It must be because you are seeking to love God with your mind. When Jesus was asked what the greatest commandment was, he answered, "You shall love the Lord your God with all your heart and with all your soul and with all your mind" (Matt 22:37). To love the Lord with your entire mind is to consecrate all the powers of your mind to deeper and greater thoughts of God. This is the noblest occupation any human mind can find. Indeed, the infinite Creator, Sustainer and Governor of this vast universe, the eternal Redeemer of his elect people, and the coming righteous Judge of the living and the dead is worthy of this. As John Mason puts it in his famous hymn, "How Shall I Sing That Majesty?"

> How great a being, Lord, is thine,
>   which doth all beings keep!
> Thy knowledge is the only line
>   to sound so vast a deep.
> Thou art a sea without a shore,
>   a sun without a sphere;
> thy time is now and evermore,
>   thy place is everywhere.

Many years after the Apostle Paul's conversion and many years into his ministry, he was still saying, "For his sake I have suffered the loss of all things and count them as rubbish . . . that I may know him and the power of his resurrection" (Phil 3:8–10). There is a yearning in the soul of every true believer to know God better. This is a result of the spiritual relationship that we have with him. This hunger is, first of all, intellectual. The mind is the gateway for the experiential knowledge of God. It is as the mind is filled with the glorious knowledge of God that the heart is inflamed with love for him and the will is inspired to serve him even at peril of our own lives.

It is this yearning that drives pastors away from everyone else to read and meditate on divine things. Those who can afford a study room go there to shut out the world so that they can fill their souls with a deeper knowledge of the things of God. Poorer pastors who cannot-afford such a luxury also need to find a place where they can go to escape the world and get yet another scoop of divine things to fill their souls to overflowing. It may be their bedroom or a shaded spot in their back yard. Wherever the place, there they will take off their sandals, as it were, and behold him who is invisible.

Reading the Bible Regularly

Your yearning for God will take you to the primary source of information about God, which is the Bible. Reading and studying the Bible will be your primary occupation. It is an amazing book. You can never exhaust it. The more you read the sixty-six books of the Bible, the more they seem to yield. Perhaps it is because your spiritual experience over time gives deeper meaning to your Bible reading and your Bible reading in turn gives deeper meaning to your spiritual experience. This spiral effect results in an ever-growing appreciation of the teachings in the Bible.

Some refer to this type of reading of the Bible as devotional reading. It is not done with sermon preparation in mind but simply because you want to know God better and your soul longs for fresh manna from heaven. Here you learn more about God and his ways. You view more of his redemptive work through the Lord Jesus Christ and his Holy Spirit. You see more of the wisdom of God in ordaining that the Christian life should be lived in the church with other believers, and so you treasure them even more. You discover more of the workings of your own heart as you see how Bible characters act and react to situations. The promises of God get sweeter as you read them afresh and apply them to current situations. Through the Bible, God continues to speak to you and to reveal himself to you.

Reading Other Spiritual Books

You will also want to read other books – spiritual books – that will help you to grow in your Christian life and in your work as a pastor. Some of these books may initially be well beyond our understanding, but the more we read to satisfy our thirst for divine knowledge, the more the contents of those books become understandable.

Such reading is a real challenge for pastors in rural areas because good books are hard to find and very expensive in relation to the average rural pastor's remuneration. However, where there is a will there is a way. You will find that pastors who are very effective in their ministries in rural areas have a small but well-used library. Their books show signs of wear-and-tear, indicating that they have been well read. Thus even relatively uneducated rural pastors can over time read good solid books and become acquainted with the deep things of God. So poverty and a lack of education are no excuse. That was why I started this chapter by stressing that the study life of a pastor is a fruit of loving God with your mind. When you do this, you will pant after God and the things of God whoever you are and wherever you are.

What is a real challenge for rural pastors is relatively easy for those who are pastoring churches in towns and cities. Although books may still be more expensive than they are in the USA and Europe, your thirst for knowledge of God should cause you to set aside some money towards building a library of good study books. When it costs an arm and a leg to acquire books, you tend to treasure them and read them!

Remember, your growing knowledge of God through personal study is an important source of spiritual power. Do not stop studying when you graduate from Bible college. Rather, you must continue to deepen the knowledge that you garnered while you were in college. It must be a lifelong preoccupation because the thirst you have for the knowledge of God must be a lifelong thirst.

Read doctrinal books. Read experiential and devotional books. Read books about the attributes and work of God. Read books about the Bible. Read books about the gospel and world missions. Read books about church history and read Christian biographies. Read books about the family and about the church. Read books about preaching and pastoral work and about the work of elders and deacons. Read the classics that have stood the test of time and continue to be reprinted. Read new books, which are hot off the press.

Are you wondering where to start? Ask an older pastor whose ministry you respect to recommend a list of good books for you to read. Let your mind continue to be fed even while you are feeding others. You will find that you have enough and to spare each time you open your mouth to instruct the people of God. There will be freshness and power in your ministry despite the passing of years. God's people will sense that you are growing even as they are growing through your pastoral preaching.

Reading for Sermon Preparation

In addition to the types of reading discussed above, you also need to be reading in relation to the sermons you are preparing. This is crucial for pastoral preaching. My approach over the years has been to study the book or passage from which the Lord has directed me to preach. I do this well in advance of starting to preach on it so that its truths have time to settle in my own mind and heart. I read and study it for my own benefit first, and then later I reread and continue to study it as I commence teaching the people of God who are under my care. It is this rereading and studying that I am speaking about in this section of the chapter.

Pastoral preaching is usually done when the whole church gathers once a week. You need to have a regular day or two in the week when you excuse yourself from other tasks, as much as possible, and give yourself to concentrated preparation for this. Study the text of your sermon afresh. Pull out all the helps that you have – the Bible commentaries, Bible dictionaries, concordances, and whatever other books are relevant – and give them due attention. Work as if everything depended on you even while you are crying out to the Holy Spirit to give you understanding and insight. Then construct your sermon, bearing in mind all that was said in chapters 13 to 15 about the different genres of texts. "Do your best to present yourself to God as one approved, a worker who has no need to be ashamed, rightly handling the word of truth" (2 Tim 2:15).

Carving out Time to Study

Anyone who has been a pastor for any length of time will know that everything that I have said in this chapter is important, and yet at the same time it is easier said than done. You will need a lot of self-discipline and patience with both your family and the church before you can get this right. Pastors with young families will often get interrupted. When kids want attention, they can get it out of a rock! You will also have to be sensitive to the needs of your spouse as you share in child care and other family responsibilities. Then there are the demands of church members who see the pastor as a jack-of-all-trades. They will call you when they need a lift into town or when Junior is running a temperature. This is especially the case in areas where very few church members own cars. The whole church then tends to think of the pastor's car as their car, and the pastor as their taxi driver. It can be very difficult to carve out regular study time in such circumstances.

However, once you realize that loss of study time is also a loss of spiritual power and vitality over the long haul, you will be prepared to pay any price to find the time for it. You can be sure of this: When your congregation is dismissed each week after hearing you preach, their sense of satisfaction and fulfilment with your ministry will, to a large measure, depend on the spiritual depth that they have sensed in your preaching. There is truly an abiding power that comes from a consistent study life, and as your congregation senses it, your relationship with them will continue to thrive.

Some pastors make a habit of reading in the early morning as part of their devotional exercises before the rest of the family wakes up. They do this as often as possible during the week. Others choose a single day when they do their weekly reading. I know of at least one pastor who, once a week, prepares a sandwich for himself in the morning, packs some good books he wants to read, and heads out to the public library in town. He spends the morning and afternoon there reading the books he brought with him, with only a short break at noon to enjoy his packed lunch. By the time he returns home, he has done enough serious reading for the week. Each of us must find the system that works best for us. There is no one-size-fits-all in developing a habit of reading and studying.

Someone once said,

> I like to think of the minister as only one of the congregation set apart by the rest for a particular purpose. They say to him: Look, brother, we are busy with our daily toils, and confused with cares, but we eagerly long for peace and light to illuminate our life, and we have heard there is a land where these are to be found, a land of repose and joy, full of thoughts that breathe and words that burn, but we cannot go thither ourselves. We are too embroiled in daily cares. Come, we will elect you, and set you free from toil, and you shall go thither for us, and week by week trade with that land and bring us its treasures and its spoils.[1]

---

1. James Stalker, *The Preacher and His Models* (London: Hodder and Stoughton, 1919), 282–283; quoted in Alexander Gammie, *Preachers I Have Heard* (Glasgow: Pickering & Inglis, 1946), 44–45 and online at: www.crosswalk.com/church/pastors-or-leadership/study-habits-of-great-men-1346275.html

Do not let your congregation feel cheated each week when they come to church only to find you empty-handed. Let them see that you are true to your calling.

Discussion Questions

1. What system of reading and study best suits your current circumstances?

2. What is the right kind of power that pastors should have in their congregations in contrast to the power that chiefs or witch doctors have over people in a village?

3. Have you recently read a book that has been like "the book of the year" for you? Why did it minister to you so much compared to all the other books you have recently read?

4. How have you managed to carve out time for reading and study, and what were the specific challenges you had to overcome in order to achieve this?

17

The Pastor's Prayer Life

Though some may question how a pastor's study life can empower preaching, almost no one will doubt that a consistent prayer life will result in a powerful preaching ministry. It is common knowledge that prayer plugs into God's power socket. The Lord Jesus Christ knew this, and so he often went out to a solitary place long before dawn to be alone with the Father in prayer (Mark 1:35). The apostles in the New Testament also seem to have known this and made it an important ingredient of their ministry (Acts 6:4). God honours the preaching ministry of those whose prayer life shows their utter dependence on him.

In chapter 10, we looked at the challenging mission that is before us as preachers and concluded that we need supernatural power to accomplish it. We saw that our task is to overcome fallen human nature, which still has a stranglehold on the souls of believers. The supernatural power of God works through us as we pray and preach the Word of God. In a sense, therefore, we have already handled the subject of prayer. In that chapter, we saw the need to ask believers to pray for us, and we also noted the need for us to pray for our preaching ministry. What I want us to do in this chapter is to look at our general prayer life as a source of preaching power and to deal with some practical ways in which we can sustain a consistent prayer life in the midst of a busy pastoral ministry.

Recognizing That Satan Seeks to Sabotage Your Prayer Life

If you think that prayer is not important to the work of preaching, I have news for you: Satan knows that it is vital, and so he will do everything in his power to stop you from praying. He is more successful at this than we care to admit. I do not know of another area of pastoral ministry that we neglect more than prayer. As I write this chapter, I feel convicted that I myself pray so little. I wish I prayed more because I know how much I need God's power in my preaching ministry. Yet I also know from being in pastors' fraternals that I am not the only one who has this problem. None of us can throw stones at one another, for we all live in glass houses as far as prayer is concerned.

Satan keeps us very busy with other things so that time for prayer is crowded out of our daily schedules. As we are waking up, he fills our minds with plans for the day and gives us the impression that those plans cannot wait and must get our immediate attention as soon as we jump out of bed. He then keeps us running all day until evening, when we are too tired to spend any meaningful time alone in prayer. He keeps this up day after day, week after week, until before we know it a prayer-less year has passed. Then we are surprised that our preaching has produced so little fruit. We were labouring while unplugged from the source of divine power.

Another way in which Satan kills our prayer lives is by encouraging us to sin against God and then laying this sin on our conscience. Usually he does this by making us engage in what we call small sins – gossiping, lying, bearing a grudge, being mean to our wives and children, and so on. Then when we try to go to God in prayer, Satan points to those same sins and tells us that we are wasting our time because God will not listen to our prayers. He gives us the impression that we will be more productive if we do something else. Thus our prayer lives slowly dwindle. We forget that God knows we are sinners and invites us to come to him just as we are. When our consciences condemn us, we must simply begin our time of prayer by confessing our sins to him. Once we have done that, God is keen to hear our other petitions.

Loving God with Your Soul

In the previous chapter I said that our study life as pastors grows out of our hunger for God as we love him with our minds. We want to know God and his ways more and more. In the same way, our prayer life grows out of our hunger for God as we love him with our souls. We want to be in fellowship with the one we have come to know in a personal, intimate way. So, although prayer is the source of power in preaching, that is not the primary motive that drives us to prayer. We simply want to commune with God as a friend communes with a friend.

Since prayer is an outlet for you as you seek to love God with your soul, you will find that you do not pray only when you go into your "prayer chamber." You will be in communion with God throughout the day. You will be interacting with him over all the affairs of your life as you go about your day. God will be your closest companion in all things. That was why people like Enoch could be described in this way: "Enoch walked with God" (Gen 5:22, 24). God was his companion in life and he often conversed with him until "he was not, for God took him" (Gen 5:24).

Finding Time and Space for Prayer

Whereas it is true that as a pastor you will be having communion with God as you go about your business throughout the day, it is still important to find time and space to shut out the world and pray. As Jesus said, "When you pray, go into your room and shut the door and pray to your Father who is in secret. And your Father who sees in secret will reward you" (Matt 6:6). We all need that place where we can "shut the door" and be alone with the one we truly love. Our heavenly Father treasures this from us as well. If we truly love God, we will want to be alone with him and so finding the time and space for this should not be a problem.

While it would be wrong to prescribe to all pastors at what time of the day they should be alone with God, it is usually wisest to do this first thing in the morning – before other things come into our lives and get us up and running. That was the wisdom of our Lord Jesus Christ in the passage we cited at the start of this chapter: "Rising very early in the morning, while it was still dark, he departed and went out to a desolate place, and there he prayed" (Mark 1:35). It was not long before his disciples found him and started pushing everyone else's agenda on him. Thankfully, having been quiet before his Father in heaven, Jesus was very clear as to whose agenda he should follow. He insisted they leave that town and go to other places so that he could preach there also. Spending time alone with God before other pressures are upon us clarifies our priorities.

You will also notice that the Lord chose a desolate (or "solitary" – NIV) place for his prayer time. We also need a place where we can be alone with God. If you have a room in your house that is set apart as a study, that is probably the best place to get away from everyone and spend time alone with God in prayer. However, few of us enjoy that luxury. In Africa, all our rooms, including our sitting room and dining room, turn into bedrooms at night. In such situations, many have found a quiet place outside the house in the backyard where they can read the Bible and pray without disturbing the people in the house. Since this is what Jesus did in the passage we are looking at, do not think this is abnormal.

The benefit of having a set time and place to meet with God is that as creatures of habit, we are more likely to maintain the practice of prayer if we do. If we do not deliberately carve out such a time, we will easily forget about prayer as a consecrated time away from everyone and everything else and will only be communing with God "on the run." As we meet with God regularly in prayer, our experiential knowledge of him grows. This will be evident in our preaching and will have an impact on those who hear us. They will sense that we do not only know about God but truly know him in a very personal way.

Maintaining a Prayer Calendar and Diary

Although this chapter is not about how to your prayer life generally as a pastor but about how to secure power in your pastoral preaching through prayer, I still want to touch on the need to maintain a prayer calendar and a prayer diary. These have been such a great blessing to my own prayer life that I must mention them. They have affected my attitude towards my preaching, my church, my family, and all my other activities and relationships.

You will notice that I am speaking about both a prayer calendar and a prayer diary. These are not technical terms. They are simply referring to tools that I use to organize my prayer time so that it covers all the important areas of my life. A prayer calendar is a schedule that covers individuals, churches, ministries, nations, and so on that I feel I have a responsibility to pray for. I call it a calendar because I repeat the cycle regularly. Currently, it covers two months, with about ten items for prayer each day, and I repeat the cycle every second month. A prayer diary is a schedule that covers specific prayer items that are brought to my attention (such as sicknesses and bereavements in the church and in the wider family, conferences and trips that are coming up, prayer requests that people share with me, and so on). When the Lord answers those prayer requests, I strike them off the list.

When I was younger and my church was smaller, I did not need these aids as much as I do now. But how else would I be able to look my more than 400 church members in the face and tell them that I pray for them regularly? I will not insist that you use these same aids, but I would encourage you to have your own system by which you organize your prayer life so that it is not solely a crisis-diffusing activity or totally at the mercy of your fading memory. Prayer must function as both an offensive and defensive weapon. There are individuals in your church who are never problematic and so, if you do not have a system that brings them to mind, they may never get much prayer attention from you. Then when disaster hits, you will feel guilty that you never prayed for them.

By this time you must be wondering how all this relate to power in pastoral preaching. It does so indirectly. A side-effect of an organized prayer life is that you start thinking about all the areas you pray for with true spirituality. For instance, praying for individual church members gives you an ongoing burden for them. You will develop a real spiritual concern for the specific areas in which they need to grow and make progress. This will feed into your sermon preparation, and especially into your applications. You will be conscious that the lesson applies to some of the people under your charge, without even having their faces before you. Your preaching will tend to scratch where your people are itching, and they will sense that they truly have a shepherd among them. That relevance in itself is power in pastoral preaching.

Praying over Your Sermon Preparation and Delivery

I dealt with the issue of praying over your sermon preparation and delivery in chapter 10 and so will not want to repeat myself here. Suffice it to say that Jesus told his disciples, "I am the vine; you are the branches. Whoever abides in me and I in him, he it is that bears much fruit, for apart from me you can do nothing" (John 15:5). We need to be utterly persuaded that the difference between a lecture and a sermon is not the eloquence of the latter but the direct work of God by his Spirit in the hearts of those who hear his Word. This fruit is secured when we abide in Jesus and Jesus abides in us. Although this is not necessarily equal to praying, one cannot speak about "abiding" without speaking about a conscious and deliberate fellowship with God. So, be much in fellowship with God over your pastoral preaching. Ask him to bless it with great power, and do this often. I cannot emphasize this enough. Prayer-less sermon preparation and prayer-less sermon delivery lead to dead churches. There are more than enough of them already. Do not add yours to that list. Pray over your sermon preparation and delivery!

Fasting

Let me end this chapter on the prayer life of a pastor with the subject of fasting. This subject is rarely handled with respect to pastoral work, and yet it is vital in securing power from heaven for God's work on earth. You will recall that once when the disciples of our Lord failed to deliver a boy from demons, the Lord explained their failure saying, "This kind never comes out except by prayer and fasting" (Matt 17:21). To be sure, fasting is not a more powerful way of twisting God's arm. Rather, it is a practice of setting aside not only our time but also our food in order to seek the Lord over issues that are very close to our hearts. We mean serious business with God over these matters, and so we want to spend more intense time seeking his face concerning them. We are so affected by the issues at hand, that we are willing to give up our daily sustenance (food) in order to keep these matters before the face of God. That is what fasting is about.

There will be times when as a pastor you will want to pray and fast. This may be prior to a series of messages that you feel very burdened about. It may be when the church is going through difficulties that all other measures have failed to address. Your spiritual consciousness is heightened as you earnestly focus on the issues you are wrestling with in prayer and fasting. That spiritual earnestness comes through in your preaching. The Holy Spirit often uses it to prevail upon the hearts of his people. Take it as a general rule that a man who prevails with God in prayer is likely to also prevail with God's children in his preaching.

Discussion Questions

1. I wrote earlier in the chapter, "I do not know of another area of pastoral ministry that we neglect more than prayer." What has your own experience been like in this area?

2. What system of organizing your prayer life has worked best for you in your circumstances?

3. What have you done to protect your time of prayer from other pressing demands in the church and in the family?

4. This chapter deals largely with a pastor praying alone. Do you have a regular time when you pray with another pastor? If so, how useful have you found this?

18

The Pastor's Own Life

"What right has he got to be standing up there preaching to us about how we ought to live when he has shown again and again that he does not live like that himself?" The enraged and outraged church member who said those words to me was talking about a pastor whose moral life had become a scandal, to say the least. Many believers feel the same way when they come to know that their pastor is not godly after all. When that happens, the effect that the pastor once had on their consciences is gone. In their hearts they say to the preacher, "Physician, go and heal yourself first and then perhaps we will come and listen to you. Perhaps."

Take it as a general rule: The day you lose your godliness is the day you lose your power in pastoral preaching. The two are inextricably connected: You lose one, you lose the other. There is no other way. Hence, it is vital for you as a pastor to be totally convinced that you must protect your walk with God and grow in godliness. In the hour of temptation, when Satan presents you with a piece of bread that is dripping with honey, remember that one bite of it may spell the end of your preaching ministry. Do not listen when he tells you that no one will know. He has said that to many others who are now on the shelf. Do not allow yourself to fall into his trap.

Loving God with Your Heart

True godliness is a fruit of loving God with your heart. If you aim for outward godliness directly, all you end up being is a hypocritical Pharisee. Outward morality can be like sticking mangoes onto a dead mango tree using a string or a tape. But you need a truly healthy mango tree if you are to harvest good, juicy mangoes. That is how it is with us human beings. Unless we love God and want to be like him, we will not sustain mere forms of godliness for long. I say again, true godliness is a fruit of loving God with your heart.

Jesus said, "You shall love the Lord your God with all your heart and with all your soul and with all your mind. This is the great and first commandment" (Matt 22:37–38). We looked at loving God with our minds when we looked at the study life of a pastor. We looked at loving God with our souls when we looked at the prayer life of a pastor. Now we are looking at loving God with our hearts as we look at the godly life of a pastor. Although this is not quite what Jesus had in mind when he quoted the words from Deuteronomy, it is a very helpful way to distinguish between these three sources of power in pastoral preaching. That way, we do not see this power as some mystical technique that gives us power over other people. Rather, we see that power flows from fulfilling our spiritual obligation as Christians. It is as we obey the great and first commandment that we continue to be truly studious, prayerful, and godly, and at the same time to be powerful pastoral preachers.

Because godliness is a fruit of loving God, those who are unconverted cannot be powerful pastoral preachers. Their hearts are still dead in sin. They love sin rather than righteousness. They may be able to preach a few "powerful" sermons before their congregations really get to know them. But eventually their true colours will be revealed. A bad smell will begin to seep through the cracks and the stench will become unbearable. The power is lost, and the sooner they leave the pulpit the better. Otherwise their churches will wilt and die. Therefore, the first issue to settle is whether you are converted or not. You cannot be godly without first having a regenerate heart.

Another reason it is vital that your godliness be a fruit of loving God is simply that motives matter to God. Many people do the right thing out of fear of being found out or out of fear of going to hell. There is nothing wrong with that, but it is the lowest level of motivation for godliness. A time comes when the power of temptation is so strong that such fear is soon overcome and sin is the inevitable result. However, when you love God you do not want to think, say, or do anything that offends him. You want to please him. This is what makes godliness sustainable.

Thomas Murphy, speaking about the pastor, puts it this way:

> It is the heart alone, and the heart glowing with love to God, that can give him strength and energy and perseverance and success. With it he will be irresistible, without it his ministerial life will be a failure. Where there is such an unction of the Holy Spirit it will, as a matter of course, impart a high and holy character; and

a character without a spot and beyond suspicion must ever be the right arm of a minister's efficiency.[1]

You Are First of All a Christian

It is vital to remember that as a pastor you are first of all a Christian. You are a sheep before you are a shepherd. Therefore, all the pleas in Scripture for a Christian to live a godly life apply to you as well. You are not an angel who comes down to earth to deliver pastoral sermons and then disappears to heaven again until the following weekend. You live in a fallen world and struggle with the remains of your own fallen nature, and so you must pursue holiness in the same way that every Christian is urged to do so. The Bible speaks to you as well as to all other Christians when it says, "As obedient children, do not be conformed to the passions of your former ignorance, but as he who called you is holy, you also be holy in all your conduct, since it is written, 'You shall be holy, for I am holy'" (1 Pet 1:14–16).

It is as you learn to apply the Scriptures to your own life that you learn to apply them to your congregation. In the home, you keep the medicines that you have found most effective in your medicine cupboard and dispense them to the rest of the family. Similarly, the biblical arguments that prevail with you, helping you grow in godliness, are the ones that you will use the most as you preach, knowing that they will most probably be effective in winning the hearts of your people from sin. The promises of God that bring you the most encouragement and hope will have a special place in your preaching when your congregation needs encouragement and hope. You can see, therefore, why knowing that you are first of all a Christian before you are a pastor is the way to knowing how to minister to your people effectively.

Your Personal and Domestic Lives

The two areas that people look at the most to see whether you really mean what you say when you preach are your personal life and your domestic life. That is why Paul emphasized these two areas when writing about the qualifications for pastoral work, saying "an overseer must be above reproach, the husband of one wife, sober-minded, self-controlled, respectable, hospitable, able to

---

1. Quoted from http://www.gracegems.org/SERMONS/The%20Real%20Power%20 of%20the%20Pastor.htm

teach, not a drunkard, not violent but gentle, not quarrelsome, not a lover of money. He must manage his own household well, with all dignity keeping his children submissive, for if someone does not know how to manage his own household, how will he care for God's church?" (1 Tim 3:2–5).

At a personal level, the people who listen to your preaching want to see a life that is characterized by the fruit of the Spirit – love, joy, peace, patience, kindness, goodness, faithfulness, gentleness, and self-control (Gal 5:22). They also want to see a high dose of humility and truthfulness in your life. It is a combination of these that produces a personal life that is above reproach and makes you faithful, sober-minded, hospitable (i.e. a lover of strangers), not a drunkard, not violent, not quarrelsome, and not a lover of money. You can be certain that your congregation is watching you to see whether these virtues are growing on the tree of your life. If they see little of these virtues as they get to know you, your preaching will lose its hold on their consciences. On the other hand, if they see more and more of these virtues the closer they get to you, be assured that a new potency will be added to your pastoral preaching.

The other area that people will look at is your domestic life. I once heard about young woman who had begun to attend a church in the town where she went to college. She found the preaching to be what she needed to grow in grace. Many times she went home powerfully affected by the preaching and resolving to make positive changes in her personal spiritual life. One day, her pastor and his wife invited her to their home after church. She was very hesitant and almost turned down the invitation. Finally, so as not to offend them, she accepted. At the end of the visit, she said to the pastor, "You know, I must confess to you that I almost turned down your invitation earlier today. This is because of my past experience. In my previous church I had a lot of respect for my pastor . . . until I visited his home. I found a home that was disorganized, the surroundings were unkempt, the children were disobedient, and the pastor spoke unkindly to his wife. It affected the way I listened to him after that. His preaching lost its power. I feared that I would be the loser for the second time if I found a similar situation in your home. I am glad that it has not been the case this time."

Some pastors try to avoid this loss of power by hiding their domestic lives from their church members. But that is unsustainable because wrong relationships in the home soon become visible in the church. Members will see what your family life must be like at home. Besides, children soon grow up. If they were mishandled in their childhood days, their rebellion in their teenage years will say it all. Worse still, when a wife files for divorce, the skeletons in the wardrobe can no longer be hidden. That is the death knell of a pastor's ministry. You can never be the effective and powerful preacher you once were when your domestic life falls apart. A pastor can never say, "Do as I say but do not do as I do." We must like Paul say, "Be imitators of me" (1 Cor 4:16; 11:1).

It is, therefore, vital to your pastoral preaching to ensure that there is true godliness in your personal and domestic lives. This will spill over into your social life The people in your community or village should tell each other, "That one is a real pastor. We have related to him and his family. We want to be like him." That is what will attract them to your preaching, and that is what will keep them coming to listen to you. Robert Murray M'Cheyne made a statement that has now become known all over the English-speaking world: "It is not great talents that God blesses so much as great likeness to Christ. A holy minister is an awful weapon in the hand of God."

Worms That Destroy Godliness

There are three worms that have often eaten away the moral fibre of pastors and thus destroyed their preaching ministries. If you are going to sustain a powerful preaching ministry for many years, you will need to watch out for these. Almost every pastoral ministry that has been suddenly cut short due to moral failure has been a victim of one of these three. Let us look at each of them.

Sex. This refers to sexual sin. John MacArthur, a well-known pastor in the USA, once said that when pastors fall they do not fall far. What he meant was that they have been playing so dangerously close to the edge of sexual integrity that the devil simply gives them a gentle nudge and they tip over. For example, there will always be some women in the church who want a close relationship with their pastor even if they know that he is a married man. The relationship can start innocently. But it can grow until it leaves the bounds of morality and finally leads to an adulterous affair. As a pastor, therefore, you need to always be on guard in your relationships both inside and outside the church. Carelessness in this area can be very costly. Many former pastors have wished they had listened to this advice.

Silver. This refers to the love of money that is a root of all kinds of evil. The Apostle Paul warned young Timothy about this when he wrote, "But those who desire to be rich fall into temptation, into a snare, into many senseless and harmful desires that plunge people into ruin and destruction.

For the love of money is a root of all kinds of evils. It is through this craving that some have wandered away from the faith and pierced themselves with many pangs" (1 Tim 6:9–10). How can we avoid this? Thankfully, the Apostle Paul tells Timothy how to do so. It is a matter of the heart. He writes, "But godliness with contentment is great gain, for we brought nothing into the world, and we cannot take anything out of the world. But if we have food and clothing, with these we will be content" (1 Tim 6:6–8). When you begin to lose this contentment and start craving for more and more of the world's goods, know that you are about to pierce yourself with many pangs.

Celebrity. This refers to the pride that comes from a ministry that is apparently successful. When your church begins to overflow and everyone seems to be talking about you, you begin to drink in the praises of people and start to believe that there is something special about you. Add to this the titles that we have begun to give ourselves such as "Man of God." We forget what the Apostle Paul said to the Corinthians, "What do you have that you did not receive? If then you received it, why do you boast as if you did not receive it?" (1 Cor 4:7). It is God who makes us successful in our work, and that is purely a gift of his grace. Knowing that, will go a long way in keeping you humble despite the obvious success that God may bestow on your ministry.

In many ways, fame is the most dangerous of the three temptations because it is the most subtle. You can see sexual temptations. You can see money and the possessions that it buys. But you cannot see pride. In fact, most proud people believe they are very humble! The biblical injunction needs to be heeded, "Pride goes before destruction, and a haughty spirit before a fall" (Prov 16:18). Beware of the pride that often attends success. It will make you less dependent on God and soon you will be an easy target for the devil.

Godly Living Reinforces Your Applications

What makes the godly life of pastors such a potent force when preaching? It is the fact that it enhances their sermon applications. Men and women will make excuses for their sin because they want to get away with the lowest level of spirituality and still go to heaven. They will enjoy a pastor's sermons as long as they are not expected to change. Yet true pastoral preaching must demand change. When the congregation do not see any examples of the kind of life that the pastor says God wants them to live, they will continue to convince themselves that such a life is impossible. But when they see in the pastor the embodiment of what the Bible demands of them, their excuses are immediately silenced. They know they have no excuse. They must pull up their socks.

A pastor's godliness also makes true spirituality attractive. Since spirituality is an outworking of loving God with your heart, the congregation will find true fulfilment in their own spiritual lives as they follow the pastor's example. Initially they might have thought that obeying God's injunctions that come through the pastor's preaching would reduce them to misery for the rest of their lives. However, when they see love, joy, and peace in their pastor's life, they are encouraged to venture in the same direction. Surely, this adds potency to the pastor's preaching.

Thomas Murphy, speaking about the effect of a pastor's godliness on his preaching, says,

> It will give such weight to the minister's words that none of them will be lost. Coming, as they manifestly do, from an honest and earnest heart, they will be received, and weighed, and remembered. It will be seen that he holds communion with God, and so men will be induced to listen to him, as otherwise they would not. The respect that his manifest godliness inspires will compel them to honour his message. And then his preaching will inevitably be clothed with double power.[2]

Another way in which godliness empowers preaching is that it energizes us in our service for God. It is godliness in the heart that makes us champions for godliness in the church and in the community. Sin is an affront to the God whom we have come to love. A soldier was once arrested for beating up a fellow soldier in the barracks. When asked why he done so, he answered, "This guy insulted my mother." That is how truly godly people feel when they see sin in the church and in the world. They take up the sword of the Spirit and engage in the good fight of faith until sin is defeated. They will do everything in their power to ensure that God is honoured not only in their own lives and home but also in their church and community.

A Godly Life Is the Fruit of Study and Prayer

Finally, it is worth stating that a godly life is normally a fruit of one's study and prayer life. The three must go together. It is as you fill your mind with the knowledge of God and walk with God in prayer that you become more

---

2. Quoted from Thomas Murphy, "The Real Power of the Pastor Is in His Earnest Godliness," n.p. Online: http://www.gracegems.org/SERMONS/The%20Real%20Power%20 of%20the%20Pastor.htm

like him in true godliness and holiness. It is as the Bible shows you the kind of God who is there that you seek to be like him and to truly obey him. On your own you cannot do it, and so you pray that he will make you like himself by the power of his Holy Spirit. It is as you study what sin does in ruining souls that you grow in compassion for those who are its victims. This not only drives you to your knees to pray for them, it also causes you to climb into the pulpit to plead with them so that they do not fraternize with sin. Your godliness will not be like mangoes attached to a tree with strings or tape but like mangoes growing on the tree. So, if you are to have true power in your pastoral preaching, love God with your mind, your soul, and your heart. Engage in spiritual exercises that undergird this love. Or, as the hymn-writer William D. Longstaff wrote in 1882,

> Take time to be holy, speak oft with thy Lord;
>> Abide in Him always, and feed on His Word.
> Make friends of God's children, help those who are weak,
>> Forgetting in nothing His blessing to seek.
>
> Take time to be holy, the world rushes on;
>> Spend much time in secret, with Jesus alone.
> By looking to Jesus, like Him thou shalt be;
>> Thy friends in thy conduct His likeness shall see.

Discussion Questions

1. What is it about our work as pastors that tempts us to forget that we are also sheep and that we need to take care of our own souls as well as the souls of those to whom we minister?

2. Are there other things besides sex, money and pride that have caused the failure of pastoral ministries that you know of?

3. It is not always easy to have a happy marriage. What particular difficulties militate against a happy marriage for you as a pastor?

4. What books or Web sites have you found most helpful in enabling you to keep an eye on your personal godliness?

Section G

The Rewards of Pastoral Preaching

19

The Reward of Seeing Believers Grow

In the early years of my pastorate, there was a man who lived on my street who was great fun to be with because he was full of humour. He had two sons and two daughters. In African culture, as in Hebrew culture, sons are more significant to parents than daughters. So he was very proud of his two sons. However, soon after his retirement his two sons died of AIDS, one after another. They had never truly been disciplined as they were growing up and, as a result, they became drunks and womanizers. The inevitable happened. They contracted AIDS and died. Their father went into a depression from which he never recovered. He too died, leaving behind a widow and two daughters. This humorous man ended his life on earth in misery. All of us who are parents dread such disappointment. When our strength is gone and our bodies are wrinkled and old, we want to be able to look at our children and our children's children and be satisfied by their conduct and character in life. We want to see that we have contributed a new generation of responsible citizens to God's world. That is the dream of any parent.

That is also the dream of any pastor. No pastor wants to look back after many years of labouring in pastoral preaching and see a church that is full of fights and quarrels, a church that is constantly appearing in the local newspapers due to its financial scandals, or a church that is the subject of village gossip because of the sexual immorality and high divorce rate of its members. That would surely break the heart of any true servant of God. Rather, pastors want to come to the end of their years of faithful labour among the people of God and see healthy churches faithfully carrying out the Great Commission, and church members who are Christlike and godly. That is not simply something that every pastor dreams of; it is in itself a reward of faithful pastoral preaching.

This is a reward the apostles also enjoyed. When you read the New Testament, you soon discover that they often rejoiced at the fruit of their labours. Think of the Apostle Paul in prison, unable to labour actively among the churches. What kept him from depression? The answer is found in his letters to the churches he had planted. He found great encouragement in reflecting on how they were doing. Thus in his letter to the Philippians, he said:

> Do all things without grumbling or disputing, that you may be blameless and innocent, children of God without blemish in the midst of a crooked and twisted generation, among whom you shine as lights in the world, holding fast to the word of life, so that in the day of Christ I may be proud that I did not run in vain or labour in vain. Even if I am to be poured out as a drink offering upon the sacrificial offering of your faith, I am glad and rejoice with you all. (Phil 2:14–17)

Paul looks forward to the time when Christ will reward his faithful soldiers and says that on that day he wants to be proud and to know that he did not labour in vain. However, it is worth noticing that, he says that he is glad even now while he is suffering in prison. It has been rightly observed that if Paul had not stated that he was in prison you would have never guessed it from his letter to the Philippians because it is so full of joy!

We find the same testimony in the letters of John, who writes, "I rejoiced greatly to find some of your children walking in the truth, just as we were commanded by the Father" (2 John 4).

This satisfaction was especially evident towards the end of the lives of the apostles. In his last letter, the Apostle John wrote, "For I rejoiced greatly when the brothers came and testified to your truth, as indeed you are walking in the truth. I have no greater joy that to hear that my children are walking in the truth" (3 John 3–4). One of John's greatest sources of joy was seeing the fruit of his labours. He saw strong churches and faithful believers, despite the persecution they were enduring. Similarly, the Apostle Paul wrote, with a note of triumph, "For I am already being poured out as a drink offering, and the time of my departure has come. I have fought the good fight, I have finished the race, I have kept the faith" (2 Tim 4:6–7). He was passing on the baton to his protégé or, to use a more African expression, he was passing on the spear to the warrior who was going to take over from him. As he did so, he was conscious that he had run his race and fought his battles successfully. This sense of joy and victory was itself a great reward.

What precisely did the apostles see in the lives of believers that brought them such joy? It is important to be clear about this so that we too can know what reward we can expect from a life of faithful pastoral preaching.

Growth in Understanding of the Faith

The first fruit that the apostles rejoiced in was the faithfulness of believers to the truths of the Christian faith. This fruit did not just appear by itself. It was a result of the work the apostles had done in instructing new believers and churches. They knew that if Christians were not grounded in the truths of the gospel, they would live very weak lives that would bring grief to the heart of God. Hence they laboured hard in pastoral preaching to ensure that God's people knew the height and depth, and the length and breadth, of the love of God in Christ Jesus.

The content of the pastoral preaching of the apostles is evident in the letters that they wrote. At the centre of those letters is the person and work of Christ. Each page illumines what Jesus has done and continues to do to save and sanctify his people. His pre-existent life, his humiliated life, and his glorified life are taught in those pages with ever-increasing clarity. Not only that, the letters explain the various fruits of the saving work of Christ – regeneration, justification, adoption, sanctification, glorification, etc. All this was being taught to believers so that they could understand what had happened to them, what was happening to them, and what God has said would certainly happen to them.

Yet the central truths of the gospel were not all the apostles taught. They knew that their work was not done until they had passed on what they called "the whole counsel of God" (Acts 20:27). As was said in an earlier chapter, they taught the believers a biblical view of God, creation, human beings, history, sin, redemption in Christ, salvation applied by the Holy Spirit, the church, the state, missions, the second coming of Christ, and so on. When these truths are taught from a biblical perspective, they together make up the tenets of the Christian faith. They shape our understanding of God's world. Once believers are grounded in these truths, they have ballast in their spiritual lives and remain stable despite the attacks of the world and the devil.

This was why the Apostle John was rejoicing in the fact that the children of "the elect lady" and his own children were "walking in the truth" (2 John 4; 3 John 4). The world is full of false teachers and false prophets. Their teachings are very deceitful. They often have just enough resemblance to Christianity to avoid being easily detected as dangerous error. Many individuals have fallen prey to such teaching and abandoned the faith. These false teachers and false prophets have split churches. Many pastors whose sermons have been doctrinally weak have found themselves with churches that are rocked with doctrinal battles leading to splits. Thankfully, as a general rule, churches that have been built upon the foundation of the gospel and good doctrinal preaching have remained stable and robust for many years. Thus one of the main sources of joy towards the end of a pastor's life is seeing how the people you ministered to have collectively attained to the unity of the faith. While other churches are fighting for their lives, you see God's people who have been under your care continuing to be united and contending for "the faith that was once for all delivered to the saints" (Jude 3).

Growth in Godly Living

Another fruit that the apostles saw and rejoiced in as they looked at the churches they had established was the godly lives of the believers. This is yet another reward that a pastor gets in this life after many years of faithful pastoral preaching. Doctrinal understanding is the foundation, and the lives of believers are the superstructure built upon that foundation. If their understanding of Christian doctrine is faulty, then the lives of Christians will inevitably also become faulty. If they have been learning sound doctrine, then their lives should soon show true godliness. These two go together. The one produces the other.

Good pastors work hard at applying their sermons to the lives of believers and calling on them to live lives that "accord with sound doctrine" in their homes, in the workplace, in the church, and in the world (Titus 2:1). In a world that is full of sin and evil, blameless and innocent lives shine like lights in the darkness (Phil 2:15). The world's godlessness and rebellion provide a context that makes true mature believers stand out. It is wonderful to hear about this and to see it with one's own eyes.

For instance, in a day when young people are moving in with each other instead of getting married and many children are being born outside marriage, it is a joy to pastor a church in which almost all the young people are waiting until they are properly wed before indulging in sex and having children. It is refreshing not only for the pastor but also for the community to see that such young people still exist.

Similarly, in a society in which many men consider faithfulness to one wife a sign of weakness and so have many wives or mistresses, it is a joy to see that the majority of the men in a church where you have practised pastoral preaching are living in monogamous marriages, being faithful to their wives, and raising godly families. You know that this did not just happen. It is the fruit of many years of cleansing the brains of these men of sinful cultural norms and replacing them with biblical truths by the help of the Spirit of God.

This is what the Apostle Paul wanted Titus to see in his later years. He knew that Cretans were "always liars, evil beasts, lazy gluttons" (Titus 1:12). Yet, he wanted Titus to engage in the kind of pastoral preaching that would produce a people who were zealous for good works (Titus 2:14). For instance, as we have seen elsewhere, he wanted the older men in the church to be sober-minded, dignified, self-controlled, sound in the faith, in love, and in steadfastness (Titus 2:2). He also wanted believers who were slaves to be submissive and do their work well rather than being argumentative and pilfering from their employers. He knew that such lives would "adorn the doctrine of God our Saviour" (Titus 2:10). If Titus laboured according to the instructions of the Apostle Paul, one of the joys he would have in later life would be seeing the godly lives of the believers in Crete being totally different from the lives of the people around them. This is a reward of faithful pastoral preaching.

Growth in Fruitfulness

The apostles also rejoiced in the fruitful lives of the believers to whom they had ministered. One of the inevitable results of understanding the gospel is salvation and a purpose to life. Once individuals are saved from sin, they are given power to overcome sinful self-centredness. They are enabled to live for the glory of God and for the well-being of others. This propels them to Christian service, and service that is done with right motives.

One of the greatest joys for a pastor is seeing this happening like clockwork after many years of labouring among the people of God through pastoral preaching. I once read a story of a pastor who was visiting a town on a preaching trip. The home where he was hosted was next to a railway track. Every so often, he would rush outside to watch a train go past, and then return to his room. His hostess asked him why he was so interested in trains. He answered, "You know, as a pastor, I find it very refreshing to see something moving without being pushed." Here was a man who was tired of pushing church members to do God's work. So for him to stand there and see this procession of railway cars go past him with nothing pushing it from behind was truly refreshing. If you labour faithfully as a pastoral preacher, bearing in mind all that I have shared in the chapters of this book, it may be your joy in later life to see God's people serving him faithfully, diligently, and sacrificially without being pushed.

True pastoral preaching has this outcome because it provides motivation. It teaches believers that there are two forces at war in this world. The forces of evil are at war against the rule of God. That war began in the heavenly places and spilled out onto this planet when Satan tempted Adam and Eve in the garden of Eden. Satan achieved a victory there, but only because God allowed it because he had a plan to show his glory by the way he would reclaim his kingdom from the evil one. Through his Son Jesus Christ and through the church, God would destroy all idolatry and rebellion and establish himself as the only true king. Believers who understand this see their salvation not simply as a way of escaping hell and going to heaven, but as being recruited into God's army to serve him in this great enterprise across history. Thus, they gladly devote their time, money, and abilities to this glorious work. In their school or workplace they deliberately work to extend God's kingdom. They support the work of church-planting missions in whichever way they can, even if they are not called to be missionaries themselves. They participate in evangelistic work. It is a joy to stand back after many years of pastoral preaching and see God's people doing this enthusiastically without being pushed. This is yet another reward of faithful pastoral preaching.

Growth in Love

Let me end with one more reward. It is the love that God's people give to one another and to you, their pastor, as a fruit of Christlikeness and in appreciation of your pastoral preaching among them. This was the experience of the Apostle Paul after he had laboured to establish the church in Philippi and then moved on to establish other churches across Europe. He later wrote:

> I rejoiced in the Lord greatly that now at length you have
> revived your concern for me. You were indeed concerned for
> me, but you had no opportunity . . . Yet it was kind of you to

share my trouble. And you Philippians yourselves know that in the beginning of the gospel, when I left Macedonia, no church entered into partnership with me in giving and receiving, except you only. Even in Thessalonica you sent me help for my needs once and again . . . I have received full payment, and more. I am well supplied, having received from Epaphroditus the gifts you sent, a fragrant offering, a sacrifice acceptable and pleasing to God. (Phil 4:10–18)

The Apostle Paul had taught this church about the importance of love as a Christian grace that believers should show to one another. Through pastoral preaching, he had laboured to turn the church in Philippi into a warm and loving family. He had taught them saying,

So if there is any encouragement in Christ, any comfort from love, any participation in the Spirit, any affection and sympathy, complete my joy by being of the same mind, having the same love, being in full accord and of one mind. Do nothing from selfish ambition or conceit, but in humility count others more significant than yourselves. Let each of you look not only to his own interests, but also to the interests of others. (Phil 2:1–4)

This love that they had been taught to express towards one another was now spilling over into Paul's own life.

Many pastors worry about how they will survive when they are too old to work and their children have left home. Here is the answer: Love the people of God and build them up in their most holy faith. As they learn to live the Christian life – which is a life of love for God and for one another – they will also express their love for you by taking care of you when you need their help. In fact, often pastors do not even need to wait for retirement and old age to begin receiving their "full payment" (to borrow the expression used by the Apostle Paul). Even while they are still serving the Lord in the church, they find that in their hour of need the church members rally round to help them. The Apostle Paul testified of this experience when he was ill while serving the churches in Galatia: "For I testify to you that, if possible, you would have gouged out your eyes and given them to me" (Gal 4:15). What a powerful expression of his appreciation of their love for him!

Many pastors have found that in their time of financial need, ill health, or bereavement, God's people, whom they have taught faithfully to live lives of love, do all in their power to alleviate their suffering. This is because they have seen the pastor's loving sacrifice in serving them and want to love their pastor back. This has been my experience and many true servants of God will testify to the same. It is truly a reward!

Discussion Questions

1. If you have already been in pastoral ministry for a few years, what signs are you seeing in the lives of God's people that are encouraging you to press on?

2. Why should seeing Christians standing for the truth in a world that no longer treasures truth be rewarding to you as a pastoral preacher? Why is truth so important?

3. What major culturally accepted practices have you seen Christians in your church stand against because of their faith, despite what their families and friends say?

4. Is there a recent testimony from a Christian (or a Christian couple) that you have ministered to through your pastoral preaching that has really encouraged you?

20

The Rewards Given by Christ

Most farming in Africa is done at a subsistence level. Families grow enough to feed themselves and sell enough to bring in some extra cash to sustain them during the year. This kind of farming is dependent on the rains. Before the onset of the rains, each family must prepare their piece of land. Soon after the first rains, they plant the seeds. Then as the days turn into weeks, they participate actively in weeding and fertilizing. In most of Africa, the understanding is that it is God (or the gods) who sends the rains and so prayers constantly go up to heaven asking for a good rainy season. Finally, the hard work is rewarded when the full harvest is brought in. This is a time of thanksgiving, joy, and praise to God. Everyone feels that it was all worth the effort. The head of the home congratulates the family for their hard work and ensures that each family member receives some money or a surprise gift when the harvest is sold.

The rewards that come to those who have worked on their farms are only a faint reflection of the rewards that pastoral preachers look forward to at the second coming of Christ. In the last chapter, we looked at the reward pastors enjoy as they see believers growing into healthy citizens of the kingdom of God. That is like the joy subsistence farmers experience each time they visit their small farms and see the plants growing and the crop ripening. They look forward to the final harvest. In this chapter we are going to be preoccupied with looking forward to the final harvest when Jesus Christ returns to reward his faithful workers. Like the head of the home, he will ensure that each one is rewarded according to what they had done.

Whereas the rewards African farmers give to family members are all eventually consumed or destroyed, the rewards given by the Lord Jesus Christ will never spoil or perish! The Apostle Paul uses a sporting metaphor to make this point: "Every athlete exercises self-control in all things. They do it to receive a perishable wreath, but we an imperishable" (1 Cor 9:25). The world's rewards are temporal and fading, but God's rewards last forever. True servants of God can anticipate a crown that never fades!

In the New Testament, the apostles looked forward to their reward and encouraged the first Christian leaders to do the same. For instance, the Apostle Peter wrote,

> So I exhort the elders among you, as a fellow elder and a witness of the sufferings of Christ, as well as a partaker in the glory that is going to be revealed: shepherd the flock of God that is among you, exercising oversight, not under compulsion, but willingly, as God would have you; not for shameful gain, but eagerly; not domineering over those in your charge, but being examples to the flock. And when the chief Shepherd appears, you will receive the unfading crown of glory. (1 Pet 5:1–4)

Notice the emphasis on "glory." The Apostle Peter spoke of himself as "a partaker in the glory that is going to be revealed" and said that faithful shepherds would in the end "receive the unfading crown of glory." The term "glory" is difficult to define and yet we all seem to sense what it involves: Honour for those who make a very notable achievement, magnificence, and beauty that fill you with wholesome pride and delight, and the splendour and bliss of life in heaven. All these are rolled up in the one word "glory." It is what Peter was anticipating, and what he wanted faithful servants of God to look forward to.

Paul expressed the same anticipation. In his letter to the Thessalonians he asked, "For what is our hope or joy or crown of boasting before our Lord Jesus at his coming? Is it not you? For you are our glory and joy" (1 Thess 2:19–20). He looked forward to his glorious reward whenever he heard about the healthy lives of the believers in Thessalonica. Even as he anticipated the approach of death, he still kept his eyes on the coming reward. He wrote to Timothy,

> For I am already being poured out as a drink offering, and the time of my departure has come. I have fought the good fight, I have finished the race, I have kept the faith. Henceforth there is laid up for me the crown of righteousness, which the Lord, the righteous judge, will award to me on that Day, and not only to me but also to all who have loved his appearing. (2 Tim 4:8)

Although the apostles engaged in many activities, preaching was their main work. Some of the preaching was evangelistic but most of it was pastoral preaching that built the lives of believers. As they saw the fruit of their preaching ministry, they rejoiced in anticipation of the rewards that their Master, the Lord Jesus Christ, was going to give them on the day of his return.

Everyone who engages in faithful pastoral preaching should have a similar anticipation of a glorious reward from the Lord Jesus Christ. This should spur us on to work even harder, just as it did Timothy when he was a pastor in Ephesus. The Apostle Paul reminded him of it when he wrote, "An athlete is not crowned unless he competes according to the rules. It is the hard-working farmer who ought to have the first share of the crops" (2 Tim 2:5–6). In other words, Paul was urging Timothy to work in a godly way and to work hard. Only those who do God's work in this way will be rewarded.

Reward and Punishment

Although the Lord Jesus Christ will reward all believers on judgment day, there will be something unique and special in store for those who have laboured in the preaching of the Word of God. James referred to it as being "judged with greater strictness." He wrote, "Not many of you should become teachers, my brothers, for you know that we who teach will be judged with greater strictness" (Jas 3:1). James immediately goes on to speak about the power our words have, comparing our tongues to the bit in the horse's mouth that allows a rider to control the animal or to the small rudder that guides a huge ship. He also wrote about the destruction that words can cause, comparing them to a spark that can start a wildfire that destroys an entire forest. Sadly, whereas we can control and tame so many aspects of nature, we find it very difficult to control our tongues so that all we say is true and honourable. James ended this section of his letter by urging all his readers to seek wisdom from God in the use of the tongue. We as preachers need to take special note that careless talk and teaching can be costly to our hearers and to us when we meet God on the final day of judgment.

It is important to keep this in mind as we engage in pastoral preaching. We must be careful what we teach, and with our words in general. The second coming of Christ will bring not only rewards but also punishment. There is no guarantee that we will be rewarded simply because we were engaged in pastoral preaching. Everything depends on what we teach and how we teach.

Rewarded for Integrity

God is not interested in teachers of his Word who do not apply what they teach to themselves. This is the highest form of hypocrisy. It is what caused the Lord Jesus Christ to issue such scathing rebukes to the Pharisees and teachers of the law in his day. He said of them,

> do and observe whatever they tell you, but not the works they do. For they preach, but do not practice. They tie up heavy burdens, hard to bear, and lay them on people's shoulders, but they themselves are not willing to move them with their finger. (Matt 23:2–4)

The Apostle Paul challenged the Jews about this same failure to apply to themselves what they were teaching the rest of the world:

> If you are sure that you yourself are a guide to the blind, a light to those who are in darkness, an instructor of the foolish, a teacher of children, having in the law the embodiment of knowledge and truth – you then who teach others, do you not teach yourself? While you preach against stealing, do you steal? You who say that one must not commit adultery, do you commit adultery? (Rom 2:19–22)

Judgment day will be terrible for those preachers who demanded very high levels of godliness in the people of God but lived in compromise and sin themselves. Their lives will be put on full display for everyone to see their hypocrisy. What an embarrassment!

There are also two other things we need to watch out for, namely faithfulness and quality. Let us look at each of these in detail.

Rewarded for Faithfulness

One of the most famous parables of our Lord is the parable of the Talents, found in Matthew 25. Jesus told this parable towards the end of his earthly ministry, when his mind was preoccupied not only with the end of his earthly life but also with the end of the world and the judgment to follow. So he told a parable about a man who was going away on a long journey and left money with his three servants so that they could use it to earn more money for him. The first two servants were given five talents and two talents respectively. They invested their talents and got returns on them. The third servant simply hid the one talent he received in the ground and went on about his own business. When the master returned, he rewarded the two servants who brought the talents with profit and he punished the servant who simply returned the one talent that had been given to him.

The words spoken by the master when rewarding or punishing his servants are very instructive. To each of those who did a good job, he said, "Well done, good and faithful servant. You have been faithful over a little; I will set you over much. Enter into the joy of your master" (Matt 25:21, 23). But he called the one who brought no returns a "wicked and slothful servant!" (Matt 25:26). The master valued and rewarded the good hearts of those who faithfully carried out the mandate they were given. The last servant had a wicked heart, which manifested itself in laziness. Hearts that God has transformed and made into good hearts will be faithful and they will be rewarded in the end.

Faithfulness has to do with faith (in fact, in the Greek language the same word is used for both). What you believe determines your behaviour. If you believe that God has called you to your work and that you must one day give an account of it to him, you will carry out that work in a way that pleases him. It will be as if God is physically present next to you, seeing everything that you are doing. That is what produces faithfulness, as the Apostle Paul well knew:

> This is how one should regard us, as servants of Christ and stewards of the mysteries of God. Moreover, *it is required of stewards that they be found faithful* . . . It is the Lord who judges me. Therefore do not pronounce judgment before the time, before the Lord comes, who will bring to light the things now hidden in darkness and will disclose the purposes of the heart. Then each one will receive his commendation from God" (1 Cor 4:1–5, emphasis added).

You will notice that he draws a straight line from the subject of faithfulness to the subject of the final judgment. The two go together. We are faithful because we know we have to give an account to God.

It is easy to be faithful for a few minutes. What is hard is being faithful over the long haul. Many individuals start their pastoral preaching ministries earnestly, keeping to the truths that are likely to build up the people of God. Then with the passage of time, they start cutting corners. In their preaching they may begin to focus on topics that will bring in the crowds, such as the promises of God, without mentioning the challenging parts such as the conditions God has laid down for the fulfilment of those promises. Their responsibility to preach the gospel and the whole counsel of God is forgotten. Such preachers may fall into the same category as the wicked servants mentioned by Jesus in another parable:

> Who then is the faithful and wise servant, whom his master has set over his household, to give them their food at the proper time? Blessed is that servant whom his master will find so doing when he comes. Truly, I say to you, he will set him over all his possessions. But if that wicked servant says to himself, "My master is delayed," and begins to beat his fellow servants and eats and drinks with drunkards, the master of that servant will come on a day when he does not expect him and at an hour he does not know and will cut him in pieces and put him with the hypocrites. In that place there will be weeping and gnashing of teeth. (Matt 24:45–51)

We need to keep asking ourselves whether we are giving the children of God their food (good food, not junk food) at the proper time. If you used to do so at the start of your ministry but abandoned that approach a few years later in order to benefit yourself, now is the best time to repent and return to what you used to do at the beginning. Remember, we will not be rewarded for the number of people in our churches but for our faithfulness to the calling God has given us.

Rewarded for Quality

Jesus expects us to serve on the basis of how he has gifted us. I am sure you noticed that in the parable of the Talents the master gave exactly the same commendation to the man with five talents and the man with two talents, despite the fact that they brought in different amounts of profit. This was because they were both working according to their abilities. Each was given the talents "according to his ability" (Matt 25:15). The man given the five talents had five-star abilities and the man with two talents had two-star abilities. When they brought in their profits, they received the same commendation: "Well done, good and faithful servant." In Luke's account they were given cities to look after according to their levels of giftedness. So, God deals with us as individuals, taking into consideration the gifts he has given us.

If we all work faithfully according to the levels of giftedness that God has given us, we may not all produce the same quantity of fruit, but we should all work to produce fruit of the highest possible quality. That is what matters most to God.

The Apostle Paul addressed the issue of the quality of our fruit when he had to deal with divided loyalties in the church in Corinth. Some church members declared themselves to be followers of Paul, some preferred Peter, others Apollos, while others claimed to be simply followers of Christ. So Paul sent them this message:

> According to the grace of God given to me, like a skilled master builder I laid a foundation, and someone else is building upon it. *Let each one take care how he builds upon it.* For no one can lay a foundation other than that which is laid, which is Jesus Christ. Now if anyone builds on the foundation with gold, silver, precious stones, wood, hay, straw – each one's work will become manifest, for the Day will disclose it, because it will be revealed by fire, and the fire will test what sort of work each one has done. If the work that anyone has built on the foundation survives, he will receive a reward. If anyone's work is burned up, he will suffer loss, though he himself will be saved, but only as through fire. (1 Cor 3:10–15, emphasis added)

The Apostle Paul urges all of us who engage in pastoral preaching – or any preaching for that matter – to be careful how we teach and what we teach. To begin with, we must all teach the true gospel so that people's lives are built on God's salvation in Christ. However, after being saved, believers will sit under pastoral preaching for the rest of their lives. If you preach simply to draw a crowd and your preaching does not really build a people for God, the day of judgment will burn up the fruit of your labours, to your own shame. However, if you have done a good job according to your level of giftedness, and your pastoral preaching has been focused on building a people for God, you will receive your reward. The message is very clear: It matters how you engage in pastoral preaching. Make sure you do it the right way because we who are preachers will be judged with stricter judgment.

The Reward Outweighs the Cost

Pastoral preaching can be very costly. Many pastors have lost pastorates because they were faithful in their preaching. Others have remained in their pastorates but have lost some church members and some friends. Why is that the case? It is because some parts of the Word of God are unpalatable to people who are self-centred and want to continue in their sins while still going to church. I spoke of congregational sins in an earlier chapter. Many people would prefer that a pastor keeps away from tackling such sins. When a pastor insists on addressing these sins, the bees soon start to sting, so to speak. Very few pastors survive this kind of conflict without emotional scars.

Then there is the financial cost. Most pastors are poorly paid. I have already alluded to the infamous saying, "Lord, keep your servant humble and we will keep him poor." The poor remuneration and resulting hardships keep many people away from pastoral ministry. This is true in Western countries, and it is even worse in Africa. Many faithful pastors across the African continent live on the verge of poverty. They may have basic food on their tables and a roof over their heads, but their clothes are threadbare and educating their children is often a nightmare. They do not even want to think about how they will survive when their strength is gone.

Think too of the cost in time and energy of wider pastoral responsibilities. Pastors spend many hours, sometimes late into the night, preparing messages, counselling individuals and couples, responding to crises, and so on. These situations can be a major drain on their physical and emotional reserves. There are many days when pastors ask the Lord, "How much longer can I go on like this?"

Pastoral ministry involves sacrifice. However, the rewards we see in this life and those that God's faithful servants will receive in eternity far outweigh the sacrifices that a pastor must make. If God allows you to reach old age after years of faithful pastoral preaching, the joy of seeing a people built for God and filling the land with the fruit of righteousness will make you say, "It was worth it!" Then when the final trumpet sounds and all of life is brought to an end, the sight of all the results of your pastoral preaching ministry will truly cause you to shout, "It was worth it!" In eternity we will be able, at a glance, to trace all the consequences of our preaching. That will be a breathtaking sight!

Many parents in rural Africa place a high value on the moral and academic education of their children. They spend precious hours teaching their children the ways of life and the ways of God. They work hard on their small farms to secure a rich harvest to pay for their children's education. They sacrifice a lot to give their children the education they never had. It is not uncommon to find aged parents with missing front teeth and wrinkled faces still living in mud huts in the village but beaming with joy as they relate what their children are now doing in the city. They can recount how much they sacrificed in order to make that possible. That is the kind of joy that fills the hearts of pastors as they contemplate the results of their sacrificial service.

The prophet Daniel recorded what he was told about the rewards to come:

> And many of those who sleep in the dust of the earth shall awake, some to everlasting life, and some to shame and everlasting contempt. And those who are wise shall shine like the brightness of the sky above; *and those who turn many to righteousness*, like the stars forever and ever." (Dan 12:2–3, emphasis added)

While "those who turn many to righteousness" does not exclusively refer to those who are engaged in preaching the Word of God, it certainly includes them. Imagine shining with the brilliance of the stars forever and ever. It will be worth all the trouble you went through in turning many to righteousness and keeping them on the straight and narrow road that leads to heaven.

Discussion Questions

1. What often discourages you as you continue in your service for the Lord as a preacher, and how can thinking about the rewards to be given by Christ help you?

2. Why do you think that the Lord looks for quality more than quantity when it comes to rewarding us for our service to him?

3. Someone once said, "Although Jesus Christ will reward us for our faithful service, we will still recognize that as an act of grace on his part." Do you agree?

4. How can thinking about your final appointment with Jesus Christ help you overcome the temptation to abuse your role as a pastor among God's people?

Conclusion

A frica desperately needs pastoral preaching that will truly build a people for God. Statistics tell us that the highest rate of quantitative growth in the church worldwide is currently taking place in Africa. However, unless there is an equal growth of spirituality, this growth will only result in wildfires, as we are already noticing around the continent. The only way we will know qualitative growth is through pastoral preaching that truly builds God's people. That is what this book has been all about.

The Apostle Paul wrote, "All Scripture is breathed out by God and profitable for teaching, for reproof, for correction, and for training in righteousness, that the man of God may be complete, equipped for every good work" (2 Tim 3:16–17). And on the basis of that he said, "I charge you in the presence of God and of Christ Jesus, who is to judge the living and the dead, and by his appearing and his kingdom: preach the word; be ready in season and out of season; reprove, rebuke, and exhort, with complete patience and teaching" (2 Tim 4:1–2). This book is a plea for pastoral preaching that faithfully expounds the Bible so that God's people are trained in righteousness. What Paul is saying to Timothy is what I am saying in this book.

I have deliberately included many Scripture passages in this book to ensure that it is not full of my own ideas about how to be a successful preacher. Rather, I want those who read this book to sense that it is describing pastoral preaching as God wants it to be. It is only as we return to God's blueprint for true pastoral preaching that we will find success as God intended success to be. As someone once said, "God's work done in God's way will never lack in God's supply." Shall I add, "God's work done in God's way will never lack God's supply and blessing"? Let us get back to the biblical way of preaching and you can be sure we will see God's blessing on our preaching as a people are built up for God.

Reading a book is one thing. Taking its contents seriously enough to do something about it is another. I am praying that those of you who are pastors or who intend to be pastors will not simply read this book, but that you will go further and make the changes necessary in your pastoral preaching that will enable you to build a people for God. Use this book as a checklist. See where you need to make changes, and make those changes now for the sake of your people. Some of the changes will not be easy and some of them will require further study. However, where there is a will there is a way. We must change if our churches are to be like hygienic homes producing healthy citizens for the kingdom of God.

If the reading of this book results in a new generation of pastors who believe the Bible sufficiently to follow its blueprint for pastoral preaching, I will feel that my labours have been adequately rewarded. I pray that their efforts will result in powerful preaching that will turn the fortunes of our continent around, as God's people mature and live God-glorifying lives in their homes, schools, and workplaces. May God indeed answer this prayer. Amen!

Scripture Index

Old Testament

Genesis
5:22, 24 157
5:24 157

Numbers
6:1–5 130

Deuteronomy
4:5 14
22:5 116
25:4 41

1 Samuel
11:27 126

Psalms
23 20
69:24–28 142
109 142

Proverbs
4:1–9 140

13:20 87
16:18 166
27:17 87

Ecclesiastes
12:13 141

Isaiah
11:9 12
51:9 115
53 141
53:2b 141
53:4b 142
53:7 142
59:1 115
61:1, 3 26

Jeremiah
1:9–10 100
2:8 20

3:15 20
10:21 20
23:1–2 20
23:4 20

Job
26:12 115

Ezekiel
33:32 105
34:1–6 20
34:11–24 .... 20, 21

Daniel
12:2–3 187

Habakkuk
2:14 12

Zechariah
13:7 21

New Testament

Matthew
4:1–11 33
6:6 157
34 115
12:39–40 127
15:18–19 120
17:21 160
22:37 148
22:37–38 162
23:2–4 182
24:6 117
24:14 12
24:45–51 184

25:23 183
25:15 184
25:21 183
25:26 183
26:31 21
28:16–20 54
28:18–20 9
28:19 10
28:19–20 37

Mark
1:35 .... 155, 157
16:15–16 10

Luke
2:14 26
10:4 116
22:31 52
24:13–27 29
24:32 .... 50, 71
24:36–49 29
24:44 .... 141, 144
46–47 10

John
3:16 134
5:39 29
10:16 19

Langham Literature and its imprints are a ministry of Langham Partnership.

Langham Partnership is a global fellowship working in pursuit of the vision God entrusted to its founder John Stott –

> *to facilitate the growth of the church in maturity and Christ-likeness through raising the standards of biblical preaching and teaching.*

Our vision is to see churches in the majority world equipped for mission and growing to maturity in Christ through the ministry of pastors and leaders who believe, teach and live by the Word of God.

Our mission is to strengthen the ministry of the Word of God through:
- nurturing national movements for biblical preaching
- fostering the creation and distribution of evangelical literature
- enhancing evangelical theological education

especially in countries where churches are under-resourced.

Our ministry

Langham Preaching partners with national leaders to nurture indigenous biblical preaching movements for pastors and lay preachers all around the world. With the support of a team of trainers from many countries, a multi-level programme of seminars provides practical training, and is followed by a programme for training local facilitators. Local preachers' groups and national and regional networks ensure continuity and ongoing development, seeking to build vigorous movements committed to Bible exposition.

Langham Literature provides majority world preachers, scholars and seminary libraries with evangelical books and electronic resources through publishing and distribution, grants and discounts. The programme also fosters the creation of indigenous evangelical books in many languages, through writer's grants, strengthening local evangelical publishing houses, and investment in major regional literature projects, such as one volume Bible commentaries like *The Africa Bible Commentary* and *The South Asia Bible Commentary*.

Langham Scholars provides financial support for evangelical doctoral students from the majority world so that, when they return home, they may train pastors and other Christian leaders with sound, biblical and theological teaching. This programme equips those who equip others. Langham Scholars also works in partnership with majority world seminaries in strengthening evangelical theological education. A growing number of Langham Scholars study in high quality doctoral programmes in the majority world itself. As well as teaching the next generation of pastors, graduated Langham Scholars exercise significant influence through their writing and leadership.

To learn more about Langham Partnership and the work we do visit **langham.org**